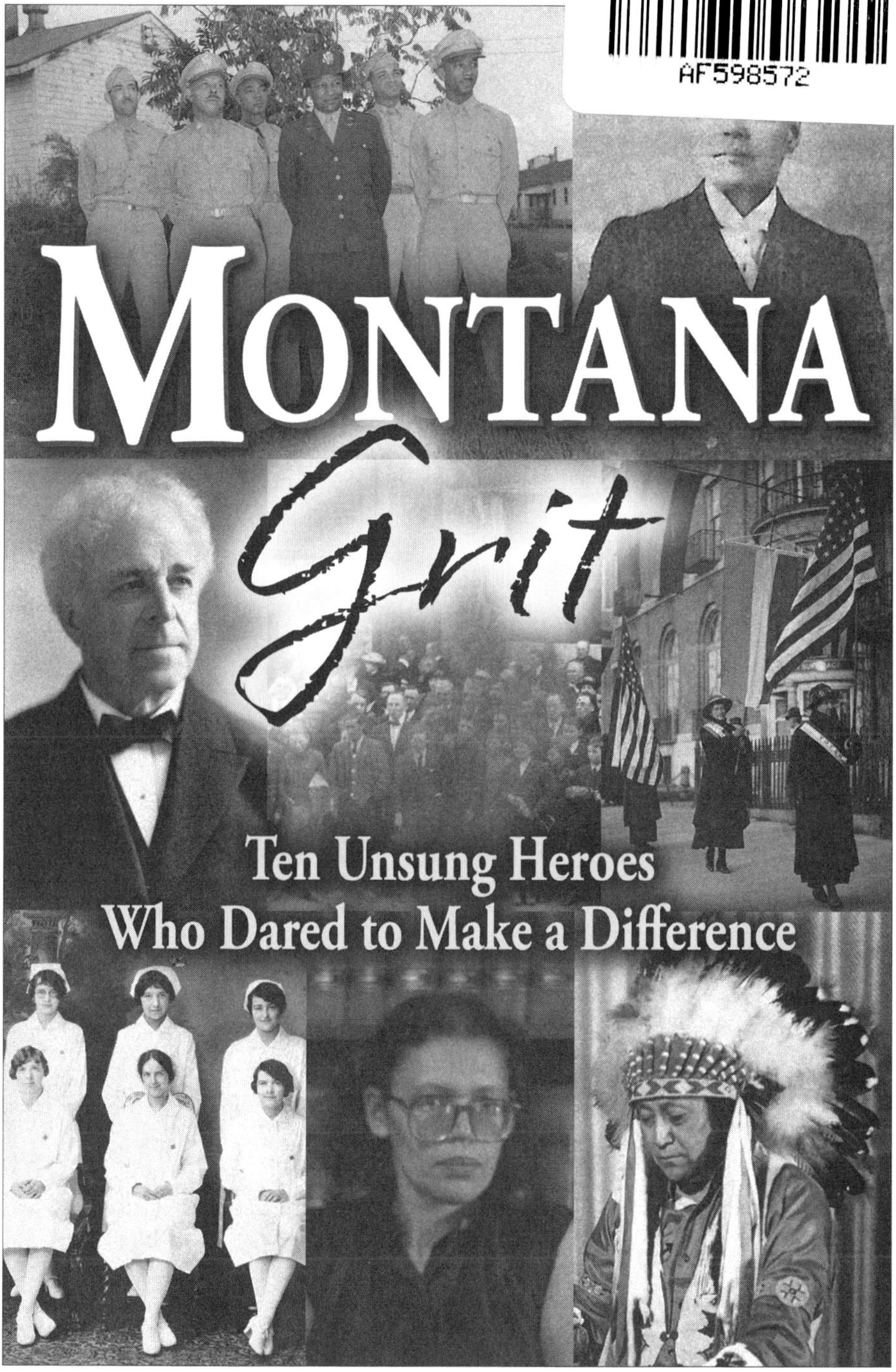

MONTANA Grit

Ten Unsung Heroes Who Dared to Make a Difference

by Marga Lincoln

Dedication

THIS BOOK IS DEDICATED TO ALL THE QUIET, AND NOT-SO-QUIET, hidden heroes and whistleblowers. We may never know who you are, but thank you.

ISBN: 978-1-56037-787-0

Design by Steph Lehmann

Front cover, top row from left: *Octavia Bridgewater photograph courtesy of Janet Harrell-Campbell; Hum Fay photograph courtesy of Butte-Silver Bow Public Archives;* ***middle row from left:*** *Judge George Bourquin photograph courtesy of the Montana Historical Society Research Center Archives; German textbooks burn in Lewistown, photograph courtesy of the Lewistown Public Library; Hazel Hunkins photograph courtesy of the Library of Congress, mnwp-160-160018u;* ***bottom row from left:*** *Susie Walking Bear (rear row, center) photograph courtesy of the Montana Historical Society Research Center Archives; Minnie Two Shoes photograph courtesy of the Sequoyah National Research Center Archives; Robert Yellowtail photograph by Kenneth F. Roahen, courtesy of the Bud Lake and Randy Brewer Crow Indian Photograph Collection, Montana Historical Society Research Center Archives.*

Back cover, top row from left: *President Barack Obama and Elouise Cobell, photograph by Pete Souza, courtesy of the White House Archives; Octavia Bridgwater photograph courtesy of Janet Harrell-Campbell; Hazel Hunkins photograph courtesy of the Library of Congress, mnwp-152-152010u;* ***center background:*** *Butte, Montana, 1939, photograph courtesy of the Library of Congress, lc-dig-fsa-8a11264.*

For more information about our books, write Farcountry Press, P.O. Box 5630,
Helena, MT 59604; call (800) 821-3874; or visit www.farcountrypress.com.

Library of Congress Cataloging-In-Publication data on file.

Produced and printed in the United States of America.

27 26 25 24 23 1 2 3 4 5

Acknowledgments

I particularly want to thank Dane Cash, associate professor of history at Carroll College, for his advice and assistance while discussing this book and reviewing several chapters, as well as providing a lot of inspiration through his excellent history classes.

A special thank you goes to Kathy Springmeyer, who encouraged me to write a book. Thanks also goes to my very patient editor, Will Harmon, whose advice, suggestions, and understanding have been much appreciated and very welcome.

I also want to thank my husband, John Hoffland, my tireless (and usually encouraging) reviewer, who also has a good eye for catching a statistic that is off base.

A sincere thank you to the following people who shared their knowledge about these historic figures:

Paul DeMain offered valuable resources and firsthand knowledge regarding working with journalist Minnie Two Shoes during their murder investigation of Annie Mae Aquash. Montana historian and writer Laura Ferguson generously shared some of her personal research information on Two Shoes and made valuable editing comments. Thanks also to Minnie's daughter, Taté Carmichael, for clarifying some facts and sending family photos. Paul Littlefield and Erin Fehr from the Sequoyah National Research Center were also enthusiastic supporters who searched for elusive photos and provided info on Minnie. Tim Bernardis, director of Little Big Horn College Library and biographer of Robert Yellowtail, provided valuable insights about Yellowtail and also shared numerous information resources.

Kevin Kooistra, executive director of the Western Heritage Center in Billings, was quick to share his enthusiasm for suffragist Hazel Hunkins and generously shared his research. He also provided information on Susie Walking Bear Yellowtail.

This book would not have been possible if Montana Historical Society historians hadn't shared their tips about their personal favorite "hidden hero" candidates. Zoe Ann Stoltz, Kate Hampton, and Martha Kohl, as well as retired MHS historians Marcella Sherfy Walter and Ellen Baumler, and MHS volunteer Bonnie Bowler, were very helpful.

I also received a great deal of help from professor Jules Harrell and Janet Harrell-Campbell, who provided information about and photos of their great-aunt "Octie," Octavia Bridgwater. A big thank you goes to Charnan Williams for forwarding her research piece in *Western Historical Quarterly* on the Bridgwater family archives, which was an incredible help in learning about the family's history. Kate Hampton generously gave editorial feedback on the Octavia Bridgwater chapter and early insights about the Bridgwater family and the history of the Black community in Helena.

John Franz was a particularly elusive person to find information about. My thanks to Fayette Miller, curator of the Frontier Gateway Museum, and Cindy Mullet for providing information and leads. Thanks also to Jason Kauffman and John Thiesen, who provided information from the Mennonite Church archives and records, and referred me to books about conscientious objectors.

Also, many helpful Montana Historical Society Research Center staff members and Lewis & Clark Library librarians were quick and efficient at tracking down stacks of research materials and books I needed.

This book would not have been possible without the support of John and Rosa. Thank you for believing in my project.

I take full responsibility for any mistakes that might have snuck into this book. I made my best efforts to catch them and stamp them out.

Contents

The Making of a Hero

Did you know that in 1917, months after the United States declared war on Germany, a mob of citizens marched through the streets of Lewistown, Montana, yanked German textbooks out of the school library, and burned them in a bonfire? In small towns and cities across Montana (and the country), a furor of nationalism turned citizens against one another. Near Glendive, self-proclaimed "super patriots" nearly lynched a minister, and in Forsyth, a mob turned on a well-respected judge. U.S. military veterans, teachers, and ministers were publicly accused of being traitors, humiliated, forced to kiss the flag, and in some cases imprisoned or almost lynched.

I first learned of these events while researching the book you hold in your hands. These were not the scenes from Montana (or American) history I'd grown up with. I was stunned. I was also fascinated and wanted to learn more.

Three of the people you meet in this book—judge Charles L. Crum, judge George M. Bourquin, and minister John M. Franz—all faced mobs during that era. Like the other people featured in this book, they had to make decisions about which side they were on. Would they join the crowd or would they hold to higher principles? Some found guidance in their love and respect for the Constitution, others in their faith.

World War I was also the time that drew the fiery and fascinating Hazel Hunkins of Billings into activism. She dreamed of being a chemist, earned a college degree in chemistry, and then learned that no employer would hire a woman. Door after door slammed in her face.

While some folks might have grown bitter, Hunkins took rejection as a call to action. This well-dressed, well-educated young woman with an engaging smile was known to scale the White House fence during some of her more flamboyant suffrage protests—no mean feat considering she wore an ankle-length dress.

Never heard of her? Neither had I.

Nor did I know much, if anything, about Robert Yellowtail, Susie Walking Bear Yellowtail, Elouise Cobell, and Minnie Two Shoes. Born on three different reservations in Montana, they each grew up facing what seemed insurmountable odds. All, at some level, grappled with the theft of their tribes' lands, resources, and power. All of them gathered their inner strength and confronted the overwhelming power, and often indifference, of the U.S. government.

Two of the unsung heroes I've gotten to know during my research for this book—Hum Fay and Octavia Bridgwater—faced racism and segregation in their everyday lives and in pursuit of their livelihoods. A boycott against the Chinese in Butte was strangling Hum Fay's once-successful business. And Octavia Bridgwater was drawn to a career in nursing, but Montana hospitals would not hire Blacks. One fought a court battle. The other lobbied the state legislature to change laws.

As I dug into the research for this book, I was struck by the fact that such strong-willed, independent, and courageous people were largely ignored by history books. Despite their grit and determination, their stories weren't widely known. I began to think of these men and women as Montana's hidden, unsung heroes. But they need not remain so. Their stories are fascinating and compelling, no less today than in their time. And they provide valuable insights into how a person faces tragedies, systemic obstacles, or major disappointments. How a person can endure. How one person can stand against fear and anger and ignorance. They are heroes because their choices and actions required courage, and they toiled not just for themselves but for the good of all.

They didn't take the easy way out.

I feel better for having gotten to know them.

I hope you do too.

And in trying times, may they inspire and guide you and me.

BOYCOTT

A General Boycott has been declared upon all CHINESE and JAPANESE Restaurants, Tailor Shops and Wash Houses. Also all persons employing them in any capacity.

All Friends and Sympathizers of Organized Labor will assist us in this fight against the lowering Asiatic standards of living and of morals.

AMERICA vs. ASIA

Progress vs. Retrogression

Are the considerations involved.

BY ORDER OF

Silver Bow Trades and Labor Assembly and Butte Miners' Union

In 1897, labor unions pasted Butte with posters urging residents to boycott Chinese-owned businesses.

PHOTOGRAPH COURTESY OF THE NATIONAL ARCHIVES.

CHAPTER 1

Hum Fay Fights Back

THE POSTERS WENT UP JANUARY 13, 1897, IN BUTTE. They blared:

BOYCOTT

A General Boycott has been declared upon all CHINESE and JAPANESE Restaurants, Tailor Shops and Wash Houses by the Silver Bow Trades and Labor Assembly.

All Friends and Sympathizers of Organized Labor will assist us in this fight against the lowering Asiatic standards of living and of morals.

America vs. Asia
Progress vs Retrogression
Are the considerations involved.
By Order of
Silver Bow Trades and Labor Assembly
and Butte Miners' Union

The result was a vise-like grip on Chinese businesses and workers that eventually drove half the Chinese population out of Butte.

The Chinese, at one time, were the largest ethnic group in Montana, making up about 10 percent of the population in the 1870 census. Approximately 1,949 Chinese lived in what was then the Montana Territory. Historians say the true number could have been 50 percent higher because the census was notorious for undercounting Chinese. By 1880, their number had declined to less than 5 percent of the population. By 1890 they numbered 2,500 but made up only 1.9 percent of residents. At that time, Butte was home to one of the largest communities of Chinese in the Rocky Mountains.

During this era, the vast majority of Chinese immigrants to the United States came from the South China delta region surrounding Canton in Guangdong Province. A population explosion in China had led to food shortages. As the Qing dynasty declined, political unrest flared, marked by rebellions, corruption, and banditry. According to historian Robert Swartout, Jr., roughly 5 million Chinese left the southern coastal area of China between 1850 and 1900, with 500,000 coming to the United States. They were lured by magical tales of "Gum Shan" or "Gold Mountain," where, as Michael Luo of *The New Yorker* writes, it was rumored a person could "pluck gold nuggets from the ground." Some moved to this country because their very survival depended on it.

By 1880, the largest groups of Chinese lived in Butte's and Helena's Chinatowns and had transitioned from working placer mines to laundry and restaurant businesses. Chinese workers also played a critical role in building lines for the Northern Pacific Railway in Montana and the Northwest.

An estimated 710 Chinese lived in Deer Lodge County, which then included Butte. Butte's Chinatown continued to grow, even after Congress passed the Chinese Exclusion Act in 1882. The act was the first federal law in U.S. history to ban entry into the country based on race nationality. By the early twentieth century, racism, boycotts, and the Exclusion Act drove most Chinese immigrants out of Montana.

The labor unions had tried to run the Chinese out of Butte before, in 1884 and again in 1891, to no avail. Then the global Panic of 1893 triggered a widespread economic depression that dragged on for years. In 1896, the anti-immigrant unions in Butte blamed the Chinese for the downturn and organized a boycott against their businesses. It was a blatant attempt to stamp out the presence of Chinese and Japanese in Butte.

But one business owner, a man named Hum Fay, fought against the prevailing racism and the unfair treatment. Originally from Sun Ning, Canton, Hum Fay is considered the driving force behind a landmark lawsuit's success in fighting the boycott. He and other Chinese community members filed a lawsuit against union leaders in Butte in April 1897 to halt the boycott that was choking the life out of Chinese and Japanese businesses.

Hum Fay remains a mystery. Very little is known about him from newspaper accounts of that time. But that's not a surprise. Much of that era's Chinese presence in Montana remains invisible. Few stories or books were written about Chinese residents' lives or work or accomplishments in Montana. In fact, they often go unmentioned in accounts of one of their greatest accomplishments—the incredibly grueling and dangerous work of building the Northern Pacific Railway. A commemorative painting by Amédée Joullin hangs in the Montana State Capitol. "Driving the Golden Spike" depicts a ceremony for the railroad's completion, with Ulysses S. Grant, railroad men, cowboys, and Crow tribal members in attendance. As historian Ellen Baumler notes, however, missing are the Chinese and Irish workers who actually built the railbed and laid the track.

A photograph of Hum Fay shows a handsome, refined young man, dressed in a Western-style business suit. A decade after the lawsuit, a reporter described him as "the mandarin of Butte" and "one of the merchant princes of the Northwest, even if he is a Chinaman." An article in the *Anaconda Standard* noted that Fay had "an unusually good grasp of English," although "his articulation is ragged."

According to a transcript of court testimony, by the time the lawsuit went to court, Fay was thirty-three and had been living in Butte for thirteen years. One of the most prominent Chinese businessmen in Butte, he owned a popular restaurant, the Palace Chop House at 37 1/2 West Park Street, which was frequented by Whites and Chinese. He also bought and sold Chinese and Japanese fancy goods.

Chinese people operated a variety of businesses in Butte, including this tea shop, the Wah Chong Tai Company, circa 1905. PHOTOGRAPH COURTESY OF ARCHIVES AND SPECIAL COLLECTIONS, MANSFIELD LIBRARY, UNIVERSITY OF MONTANA.

The boycott severely impacted him as well as several hundred Chinese in Butte. Nearly 300 Chinese signed a petition supporting Fay's lawsuit and contributed $20 each to the legal fight.

They decided to take their grievances to court despite the pervasive hostility of the Montana courts toward protecting Chinese legal rights and the indifference of local police and legal authorities to protect them. By the time the boycott ended, half the city's population of Chinese, an estimated 350 residents of 700, had left Butte.

As Mark Johnson reports in his book, *The Middle Kingdom Under the Big Sky: A History of the Chinese Experience in Montana*, nearly 300 Chinese signed the petition supporting the suit despite being warned not to sue by the powerful Chinese Six Companies in California, which advocated nationally for Chinese in America. They advised, "You are crazy to go against labor unions and the American law."

The Butte Chinese ignored the advice and hired Wilbur Fisk Sanders as their attorney. A highly esteemed Helena jurist, Sanders initially found fame as a vigilante tracking down the infamous Plummer gang and had served one term as a U.S. senator. For much of his career, Sanders was a staunch defender of racial equality.

Wilbur Fisk Sanders proved to be an effective advocate for Chinese business owners. PHOTOGRAPH COURTESY OF ARCHIVES AND SPECIAL COLLECTIONS, MANSFIELD LIBRARY, UNIVERSITY OF MONTANA.

In the 1890s, Butte's Chinatown was thriving in the city's central business district and was home to three large restaurants, numerous laundries, stores, a tailor shop, and at least two doctors. Chinatown's boundaries were Main Street on the east, Galena Street on the north, and Mercury Street on the south.

As soon as the boycott posters went up in January 1897, strong-arm tactics and threats began. "Delegates," a euphemism for what were actually enforcement thugs, targeted Chinese and Japanese businesses, Chinese and Japanese workers, and any White citizens and businesses that hired these workers or were customers of the targeted businesses.

This was not the first time unions had launched a boycott against the Chinese. A previous 1891–1892 boycott was a miserable failure, but one that the planners learned from. This time around they came back with much more oppressive and far-reaching tactics.

HATRED AND HOSTILITY AIMED AT CHINESE

The animus toward the Chinese dates back further than 1891, however. In 1884, flyers had circulated around town ordering Chinese residents to leave Butte. They ignored the demand.

Unions resented immigrants and supported immigration restrictions, seeing newcomers as competitors for jobs. They also blamed downturns in the economy on the outsiders, who were faulted for working for low salaries. However, unions refused membership to Chinese workers, so there was no practical means for Chinese workers to organize and demand higher pay.

It was a frightening time to be Chinese in Montana and the American West. When the Federal Exclusion Act passed, it was a further green light for racist behavior and racial violence targeting Chinese. Journalist Michael Luo writes that on November 3, 1885, vigilantes in Tacoma, Washington, forced 200 Chinese to leave the city in pouring rain, herding them onto passenger trains, into boxcars, or to leave town on foot, walking along the railroad tracks to Portland 140 miles south.

Years earlier, in Shasta County, California, White miners attacked a group of Chinese miners, marching seventy-five workers through the town's streets where the Chinese were pelted with stones. The sheriff freed the miners, but despite this, vigilantes rampaged through Chinese mining camps. The rioters were arrested, but all were acquitted.

Luo also describes an 1871 attack, when a White mob raged through the streets of Los Angeles' Chinatown, ransacking, looting, and lynching Chinese, leaving twenty dead including a fourteen-year-old boy. In 1877, White rioters stormed San Francisco's Chinatown, setting buildings on fire, looting, and assaulting residents. Four people were killed and fourteen wounded.

That level of violence never exploded in Butte, but in a 1901 letter to Congress, the Chinese minister, Wu Ting-Fang, outlined "damages" suffered by Chinese from 1886 forward and cited "the secret murder of a number of Chinese" in Butte, which was attributed to "the spirit of lawlessness and hatred created by" the boycott conspiracy.

While the 1891 Chinese Boycott in Butte had fizzled out, these new boycott organizers were more systematic in their tactics. They secured a huge buy-in from a large network of unions, with more than twenty endorsing it. Eventually, as many as 3,000 union conspirators and some business owners participated in the boycott. It is not clear that the Butte citizenry embraced the boycott, but locals were threatened and bullied and harassed into honoring it.

The boycott plotting began in late 1896 and involved the Cooks and Waiters Assembly, the Hotel and Restaurant Keepers, and major steam laundry proprietors. These unions contributed money to cover the cost of flyers and banners and payment for "walking delegates," who basically enforced the boycott. The baker, hard-rock miner, and musicians' protective unions also joined the boycott, even though few Chinese were working in those trades.

A newspaper announcement proclaimed: "By order of the Silver Bow Trades and Labor Assembly, American manhood and American womanhood must be protected from competition with these inferior races and further invasions of industry and further reductions of the wages of native labor by the employment of these people must be strenuously resisted."

In "Boycott in Butte," an article in *Montana, The Magazine of Western History*, Stacy Flaherty writes that the unions considered the Chinese "an inferior and backward people and, therefore, morally, economically, and socially undesirable." This was their rationale for driving the Chinese out of the community and the state.

An editorial in the February 11, 1893, *Butte Bystander*, the newspaper for the Silver Bow Trades and Labor Assembly, is but one example of their vitriol:

> **The Chinaman's life is not our life; his religion is not our religion. His habits, superstitions, and modes of life are disgusting. He is a parasite, floating across the Pacific and thence penetrating into the**

interior towns and cities, there to settle down for a brief space and absorb the substance of those with whom he comes into competition. His one object in life is to make all the money he can and return again to his native land, dead or alive. His very existence in our midst is an insult to our intelligence. Pestilence and disease follow in his wake, no matter what sentimentalists say to the contrary. Let him go hence. He belongs not in Butte.

Historians have traced some of the anti-Asian sentiment to the protracted economic downturn in the mid-1870s, which fanned White resentment and anger, but Asian newcomers had nothing to do with the broader economic troubles or the hardships Americans faced during that time. As Montana historian Robert Swartout, Jr., points out, Asians were typically working in jobs that Whites did not want. More to the point, outright racism was prevalent.

The Japanese were lumped in with the Chinese during the boycott. The January 17, 1898, edition of the *Butte Bystander* argued that the Japanese posed the same threat as the Chinese:

The Japs don't become American citizens any more than the Chinese and their mode of living is not entirely unlike that of the latter class. That they are just as bad at cutting wages and lowly living is demonstrated in Tacoma, Washington. Furthermore, they are as cute as rats, and it is just simply impossible to get rid of them.

As Flaherty notes, "[T]he labor press contributed deriding comments on Chinese businesses, labeling Chinese laundries 'pest houses' and Chinese laundrymen as 'leperous [*sic*] and mouth-spraying.'"

Boycott organizers apparently saw themselves as gallant protectors of Butte womanhood, arguing that Chinese workers were displacing "unemployed

White girls," thus forcing local women to seek work as prostitutes. Ironically, the Chinese boycott was actually preventing a number of Butte women, specifically the keepers of boardinghouses, from surviving. Several of them had Chinese employees who they wanted to keep on as staff. The boardinghouse owners quickly became targets of abuse and harassment.

BOYCOTT TACTICS

Attacking Chinese went beyond degrading articles and editorials in the local newspapers. According to Flaherty, the unions put anti-Chinese banners on a wagon float that featured insulting pictures of Chinese laundrymen spitting on the clothing they were cleaning and showing a Chinese baker about to drop a rat into dough he was making. Union men drove the bannered wagon all over Butte, including Chinatown. A gong was sounded to draw the public's attention. A local Chinese merchant later testified that he found the pictures on the wagon to be insulting and abusive. Flaherty writes that the unions "used tactics designed to ridicule and intimidate both Chinese and Japanese residents, employers of Asians, and patrons of Asian businesses."

The unions' so-called "walking delegates" stationed themselves for days at a time at the doors of Chinese and Japanese businesses. They physically blocked customers from entering restaurants and stores, turning them away and threatening them. One such customer was John A. Leggatt, a mining engineer, who was confronted as he entered Hum Fay's Palace restaurant. Leggatt testified that he saw men standing outside the restaurant who were telling people to not go in because they were boycotting the Chinese. When they confronted him, he said, "I told them to go to Hell."

"Chinese merchants and restaurant operators were the main targets of the boycott," writes Flaherty. "[O]wned by the wealthiest of the Asians," these businesses "represented the real potential for success among the Chinese and Japanese."

The unions' thugs followed Chinese laundrymen on their rounds as they picked up or delivered laundry to Butte homes. The thugs would then intimidate residents into honoring the boycott. They did the same to customers of a successful vegetable gardener. They also went to homes where Chinese cooks, gardeners, or servants were employed and pressured the residents to fire their employees.

Flaherty cites direct pressure on Thomas Fletcher, who worked as a teller at W. A. Clark and Brothers Bank. Thugs told Fletcher to fire a Chinese employee and place a White woman in the job. A "delegate" pushed the boycott at the bank and also went to Fletcher's home and spoke to his wife. Boycotters also urged customers to withdraw their money from the bank, hurting business until the banker agreed to their terms.

Flaherty documents harassment of lodging-house keepers who had Chinese employees, whom delegates insisted be fired. Mrs. Margaret Noyes refused to fire her Chinese cook, Sam. Boycott enforcers distributed flyers around the neighborhood to pressure her. Many of her boarders were union members. She eventually fired Sam and was forced to pay a fine to cover the cost of the flyers. After she sold the business, moved, and started a new business, she was harassed there as well.

Boycotters also targeted Mrs. Eva Althoff, who hired Chinese workers at Will House, her boardinghouse. She stood up to the boycott and threatened legal action against the Silver Bow Trades and Labor Assembly and Butte Miners' Union. She asked Mayor William Thompson for police protection, but he refused. Boycotters harassed her boarders. Some were told their businesses would be boycotted, others that they'd be fired. Eventually, she too was forced to go along with the boycott.

The boycott's damage to both Chinese business owners and workers was devastating, with businesses suffering catastrophic declines in income. Vegetable grower Lock Jim went from daily sales of $30 to $40 to few if any sales each day. Cooks, laundrymen, and laborers were fired.

The business owners turned to the mayor and the police for help. Since they had paid business license fees and taxes to the city, they expected some police protection. But city officials claimed there was nothing they could do and told them to "get a good lawyer, and arrest them." In fact, the city council endorsed and approved the boycott conspiracy. And the state attorney general, H. J. Haskell, found nothing wrong with the boycott, which he communicated in a very insulting letter. He wrote that American diplomacy had yielded "us an inheritance of Mongolian vampirism, which has fastened itself upon every source of living common to American wage workers." Haskell denied that the need "to remove this human barnacle by lawful and legitimate measure" violated any treaty obligations.

On behalf of a Japanese business, however, the Japanese Consulate stepped in and complained to the State of Montana, which resulted in Butte officers giving a Japanese restaurant police protection.

The only recourse for the Chinese was to take the case to court, where there was no assurance of victory. Fortunately, they had hired an excellent attorney in Sanders.

Hum Fay, Dr. Huie Pock, Dear Yick, and Hum Tong filed a lawsuit April 15, 1897, *Hum Fay et al v. Baldwin et al*, against twenty-two defendants who were the leaders of the boycott and businesses benefiting from it. The plaintiffs alleged unlawful and malicious conspiracy to deprive the Chinese of the privilege of doing business and of equal protection of the laws and denying them rights secured by laws and treaties of the United States. They asked for an injunction to stop the boycott and also for damages of $50,000. The fact that the Chinese turned to the courts seeking justice shows remarkable trust in the American justice system.

During Montana's territorial years, "Montana courts listened to Chinese complaints, recognized their seriousness, and judged them equitably," wrote historian John R. Wunder. By the mid-1880s, however, after the Federal Exclusion Act passed, Wunder said, "Montana justices seemed to reflect popular attitudes toward the Chinese. The court became anti-Chinese, too." Among the injustices that the Montana Supreme Court allowed to stand were laws preventing Chinese from buying mines, a poll tax targeting Chinese miners, and a discriminatory laundry tax on Chinese laundry owners.

Assisting Sanders in the case was his son, James U. Sanders, and Francis Brook. And defending the accused were Butte attorneys Josiah L. and Melvin I. Wines. The presiding judge was Hiram P. Knowles, whose reputation was that he was no friend of the Chinese. Knowles had been an associate justice on the Montana Territorial Supreme Court from 1868 to 1879, and in every case with Chinese litigants, he wrote the majority opinions against them.

Knowles appointed Henry N. Blake to be Master in Chancery to assist the court in gathering facts, which, according to Flaherty, was a common step in complicated court cases. Knowles also granted a temporary restraining order to halt the boycott on April 16, 1897. The case was to go to a hearing May 10 but was postponed until 1898.

Sanders' team built a meticulous and compelling case, calling 100 witnesses. He set out to prove that a boycott existed and that it caused significant damages to the Chinese. The witnesses testified to the vicious tactics used and also the devastating impacts on their businesses. When asked how much his business had decreased once the boycott started, Hum Fay testified, "Pretty near all fallen off. In the summer of 1896, I sold three or four hundred meals a day." After the boycott started, Hum Fay said, "I only sell four or five dollars a day, that is all."

Hum Fay's neighbor concurred, describing what he saw:

> **Used to be he done a good business before the boycott, but afterwards, as soon as these walking delegates kept there in front of his house, and I believe that his business dropped nine out of ten. There is hardly anybody there at any time I come in there at noon time; used to be a full house at the noon hour before the boycott.**

—∞—

Blake reported in his twenty-nine findings of fact that some union members had used force to prevent customers from doing business with the Chinese and that public officials failed to protect the Chinese.

On May 18, 1900, Judge Knowles issued a final decision in favor of the Chinese plaintiffs. He made the injunction permanent. He also awarded $1,750.05 for legal fees. However, the win was but a partial victory. The Chinese, who had endured so much loss and humiliation, had sought $50,000 in damages but received no compensation. The defendants were apparently broke.

The May 19, 1900, edition of the *Daily Intermountain* opined that the decision was "far-reaching" and "sweeping," and "calculated to make the Chinese immune from harm." When the plaintiffs won, the Six Companies in California reportedly stated, "The Butte Chinese are the smartest anywhere in the United States."

The Chinese plaintiffs would later take their request for damages to the U.S. government, asking it to make good on its treaty obligation and detailing all the times the government had failed to protect them. They requested $500,000 to cover five years of financial losses. Their request was denied. Secretary of State John Hay, in dismissing the case, actually had the gall to chastise them for not taking action sooner.

Following the boycott defeat, there was an uneasy peace for the next two decades, coinciding with Butte's greatest prosperity, according to Butte's Mai Wah Society. Public opinion mellowed. In 1906, the *Anaconda Standard* included a complimentary article about the Chinese, writing, "They care for their own people and don't burden welfare." It reported that Chinese were becoming Americanized and Christian. "Society people in Butte have made the Chinese noodle parlors popular places to eat and Chinese truck gardens on the flat provide the city with fresh produce. They measure up well to other foreign groups in town and are definitely more peaceful."

In a February 5, 1911, article in the *Anaconda Standard*, the reporter sought out Hum Fay and described him holding "forth in a big, three-story brick structure at the corner of Colorado and Mercury streets, where he conducts a general mercantile and restaurant."

On March 24, 1912, the *Butte Miner* reported a well-attended gala dinner serving delicious Chinese dishes such as "birds' nest pudding, chop suey, fish in every form and variety" and much more. The county attorney, sheriff, undersheriff, and a professor at the State School of Mines were among those attending this first annual banquet celebrating the new Republic of China.

In 1909, the Butte *Daily Post* described Hum Fay's wedding to Miss Chew Gum Ah Yen of Spokane, Washington, beneath the headline, "Wedding of Chinese Belle and Butte Merchant to Be a Real Swell Affair." The article describes Miss Ah Yen as the daughter of "one of the wealthiest merchants of the Chinese colony" of Spokane. She received "a thorough common school education in the public schools of that city and is a graduate of the Blair business college in the inland empire metropolis." The story continues with similar approval for the groom: "Hum Fay is 38 years of age and has for years been engaged in the mercantile and restaurant business in this city, being a leader among his people and undoubtedly the most popular Chinese man in the Northwest."

The wedding caused quite a stir because Chinese weddings in the United States were so rare primarily due to the Chinese Exclusion Act.

Fay was apparently a practicing Baptist, and a Baptist minister presided at the wedding. The *Anaconda Standard* reported, "He is a handsome Chinaman, having cultivated all the refinement of an educated American, quiet in manner, deferential alike to friend or stranger, keen in business, respected by all classes, and the possessor of considerable wealth."

The future looked bright for Hum Fay, but that was not to be. Exactly what went wrong in his life isn't clear, and little more appears in the newspaper record. Somewhere along the way, his marriage disintegrated. A few small articles give some puzzling details.

In February 1923, Fay was charged with vagrancy, and a short 1924 article notes that he was charged $25 for conducting a gambling game. But there's little that prepares one for an article in the *Montana Standard* on April 22, 1932, with the gleeful headline "Pauper's Grave Will Claim Body of Chinese 'Big Shot' in Halcyon Days of Butte."

Fay died at the county poor farm "alone and friendless" with no one to claim his ninety-pound body. The newspapers blamed a profligate lifestyle. According to the *Montana Standard*, he had run a gambling house worth $200,000 at one time. Perhaps Fay suffered irreversible losses during the hard times. The full truth of what happened went to the grave with him.

Hum Fay had lived at the poor farm for ten years prior to his death. He was buried in the pauper's field at Butte's Mountain View Cemetery.

THE ANACONDA STANDARD: SUNDAY MORNING,

CHINESE BUSINESS MAN OF BUTTE AND HIS BRIDE MARRIED BY BAPTIST CLERGYMAN AT GROOM'S HOME

MISS AH YEN OF SPOKANE

HUM FAY OF BUTTE

Photos by J. H. Hinton Studio.

Announcing their marriage, the January 17, 1909, the Anaconda Standard *featured portrait photographs of Hum Fay and Ah Yen.* PHOTOGRAPH COURTESY OF BUTTE SILVER BOW PUBLIC ARCHIVES.

CHAPTER 2

Defending the Constitution Against Paranoia and Hysteria: Judge Charles L. Crum

THE POLITICS OF FEAR ARE NOTHING NEW IN THIS COUNTRY, or in Montana. More than a century ago, in January 1918, a county district attorney tried to physically attack a district judge in the Montana State Capitol after the attorney lost his case in court.

As Rosebud County District Attorney Felkner F. Haynes advanced toward judge Charles L. Crum of Forsyth, accusing him of being pro-German, Crum pulled a revolver from his pocket and stopped Haynes in his tracks. But this confrontation was just a prelude of more ugliness to come, with Haynes as ringleader.

This scene is but one alarming snapshot in a Montana drama that would unfold in Forsyth and the state capitol over the coming months. It would ruin the career of one of the men and sully the reputation of Montana for decades. After the United States entered World War I in April 1917, so-called "super patriots" unleashed vigilantism and mob violence against their neighbors and even their friends in Montana and across the country.

Fear and hysteria led to unjust accusations against hundreds of Montanans, often immigrants, of being unpatriotic. The result ranged from imprisonments, ruined lives, and broken families to lost livelihoods, lynchings, beatings, public humiliations, and murders. Powerful corporate interests, particularly the Anaconda Company in Butte, would use the war effort and "patriotism" to accuse union workers and union organizers of sedition and espionage as a means to crush the labor movement.

Peace groups, political reformers such as the Progressive Party and the Nonpartisan League, and pacifists would likewise come under fire as being unpatriotic. And, of course, those who were foreign born, particularly those of German heritage, suffered intense discrimination and hostility once the United States declared war. Montana author and historian K. Ross Toole wrote of this period, "No state in the union engaged in quite the same orgy of book burning, inquisition of suspected traitors and general hysteria."

Crum would be caught up in this feverish maelstrom sweeping across Montana by merely following his heart and his belief in the Constitution's guarantee of the right of free speech. As a judge, he would refuse to be swayed by the hysteria, thus earning him the enmity of powerful adversaries.

Historian Dave Walter wrote extensively about Crum, piecing together his history by working with Crum's descendants seventy years after these dramatic incidents.

When Crum, a native of Indiana and of German-American descent, first moved to Montana in August 1906, it must have been with hope and optimism in his heart. He and his wife, Jessie, with their three young sons, homesteaded near Sanders in what was then Rosebud County (since partitioned into Treasure County) in hopes that the dry climate would improve Jessie's fragile health. They filed for a farmstead in the Yellowstone Valley between Hysham and Sanders and started raising sheep. Crum also opened a storefront law office in Sanders. Within a short time, they built a cabin, barn, corrals, sheep sheds, and more than two miles of fence on their farmstead. He acquired a patent for the land in 1909.

Crum's considerable career achievements indicate he was bright, energetic, and ambitious. Just thirty-two years old when he arrived in Montana, he had already seen success in his law career. At age twenty, Crum had moved from Wilmot, Kansas, where he had grown up, to El Reno, Oklahoma Territory, where he took a job as court reporter. He studied law with a local attorney and soon passed the bar exam. At age twenty-two, the young lawyer married seventeen-year-old Jessie Helen Mitts. Then in 1901, at just twenty-seven, Crum was elected to a judgeship in El Reno.

Between 1897 and 1905, the couple had three sons: Charles Liebert II, Claude, and Maurice. Jessie was pregnant when she and Crum homesteaded in Montana in 1906. Two months later, Dorothy was born. And in 1909 a son, Frank, followed. Jessie's health continued to decline after Frank's birth, spurring Crum to move the family to Forsyth, the seat of Rosebud County. In 1910, Jessie died at age thirty-one, leaving Crum a widower at just thirty-six, with five young children to raise; the oldest was thirteen.

Despite the personal trauma of Jessie's illness and death, Crum excelled in his law practice. "Crum's abilities quickly earned him a reputation as an efficient, diligent, and conscientious attorney," wrote historian Dave Walter. In 1911, Crum was elected Rosebud County Attorney as a Republican. As Walter noted, the *Forsyth Times-Journal* wrote of Crum, "He is not a grand-stander or a hot air merchant, but a safe and conservative lawyer of the popular 'old school.'"

In 1913, at the age of thirty-nine, Crum was elected as judge of the 13th Judicial District Court, which included the three-county area of Yellowstone, Carbon, and Rosebud. Two years later, he was elected as judge of the newly created 15th District.

"The reputation that Judge Crum built during his first term proved stellar," wrote Walter. When Crum ran for the judgeship of the 15th District, he was unopposed. Walter's research revealed further support from the editors of the *Forsyth Times-Journal*:

> **There is no man on the bench in the State of Montana that has attained a more enviable record in the few short years that he has been there than has the Honorable Charles L. Crum. . . . There is no judge on the bench today that is held in higher esteem than is Judge Crum by the members of the bar who have had occasion to transact legal business before his court.**

> **Knowing the high standing of this man, those who would have otherwise aspired to this office have sidetracked the job this fall and are all lined up behind Judge Crum to a man.**
>
> **While he has no opposition in the field, he is appreciative of the good will of the people toward him and will, in the future as he has in the past, administer justice fairly and impartially to everybody.**

Crum's career and esteem in the community was at its pinnacle, but all of that would crumble. Within two years his reputation was in ruins. The tale of his downfall began when, after years of U.S. neutrality and citizen opposition to any foreign entanglements, the United States declared war on Germany on April 6, 1917.

WAR COMES

The Great War broke out July 28, 1914, with France, Russia, and Britain on one side (the Allied Powers), facing off against Germany, Austria-Hungary, and initially, Italy (the Central Powers).

Americans were divided over whether the United States should join the Allies. Many Americans had strong ties to the Central Powers. As historian David Kennedy wrote in *Over Here: The First World War and American Society*, "One of every three Americans in that year [1910] had been born abroad or had at least one parent born abroad. Of those thirty-two million persons from families with close foreign ties, more than ten million derived from the Central Powers."

Montana mirrored national trends. According to the 1910 federal census, 54 percent of Montanans were foreign born or children of immigrants. Only 46 percent of Montanans had parents born in the United States.

When the United States finally entered the war in 1917, it did so reluctantly, and only after a series of provocations. German submarines indiscriminately sank U.S. merchant ships in the Atlantic Ocean, and then British intelligence intercepted a German telegram entreating Mexico to attack the United States as a way to regain control of Arizona, New Mexico, and Texas.

Americans were outraged but fearful. Five million soldiers had already died on European battlefields in the first two and a half years of the war. Although many Montanans had initially opposed the war, 10 percent of its population, or nearly 40,000 people, would end up enlisting or being drafted. Montana had the highest percentage of citizens serving in the military compared to other states, exceeding all others by 25 percent. This was partially due to a census mistake that almost doubled the state's actual population.

If emotions weren't already riled enough, President Woodrow Wilson further inflamed anti-German sentiments in his April 2, 1917, declaration of war speech to Congress when he spoke of "millions of men and women of German birth and native sympathy who live amongst us." While most were loyal to the United States, Wilson warned, "If there should be disloyalty, it will be dealt with a firm hand of repression. It is a fearful thing to lead this great peaceful people into war, into the most terrible and disastrous of all wars, civilization itself seeming to be in the balance."

Americans were not eager to go to war. It was just fifty-three years since America's Civil War had ended. And some congressional members, such as Civil War veteran Isaac Sherwood of Ohio, vividly remembered the slaughter and refused to vote for the war. He was joined by Montana pacifist Jeannette Rankin, the first woman elected to Congress, who addressed the House through tears, saying, "I want to stand by my country but I cannot vote for war. I vote no."

Altogether, six senators and fifty representatives voted against the war. North Carolina Representative Claude Kitchin predicted at the time, "For my vote I shall be not only criticized but denounced from one end of the country to the other. The whole yelping pack of defamers and revilers in the nation will at once be set upon my heels."

President Wilson was deeply involved in spreading "the bacillus of fear," according to historian David M. Kennedy. "Xenophobia was not new in America in 1917, but the war opened a wide field for its excesses." Among these excesses was Montana Governor Sam Stewart's appointment of a Montana Council of Defense (MCD), with encouragement from President Wilson and the Council of National Defense. In turn, the MCD established county and community councils with quasi-legal authority.

At first, these councils promoted boosting agricultural production, but they soon turned their attention to targeting those they identified as "slackers" or those suspected of having pro-German views. "Rapidly the line of

Members of the Montana Council of Defense included the governor, S. V. Stewart, and Helena Independent *publisher Will Campbell.* PHOTOGRAPH COURTESY OF THE MONTANA HISTORICAL SOCIETY RESEARCH CENTER ARCHIVES.

appropriate patriotism was crossed and attacks on 'un-American activities' began," wrote Walter.

In their super patriotic zealotry, local councils' actions ran the gamut from the terrifying to the absurd. In Glendive, a vigilante group that included the local sheriff and at least one prominent attorney almost lynched a pacifist Mennonite minister (see Chapter 4 on John Franz).

The councils also decreed that sauerkraut would now be called "liberty cabbage," and hamburger was dubbed "liberty steak," recounted Walter. In Brockway, an overzealous teacher cut all the German words and any German songs from textbooks and song books, even removing German flags from the dictionary.

The situation grew even worse when in an "Extraordinary Session" in February 1918 the Montana Legislature gave the MCD powers equivalent to that of a state agency. The MCD promptly issued seventeen orders, including outlawing use of the German language in schools, churches, and books; prohibiting burning from June through September; and forbidding dances or charity benefits without written permission from the council.

On a more ominous note, the MCD now had the power to investigate anyone it wanted to and decide on a punishment, without any chance for the accused to appeal. Any infractions were considered a misdemeanor and punishable by not more than a year in jail or a fine not to exceed $1,000 or both. It was the perfect ticket to promote bullying and vigilante injustice of the worst kind. Before long, incidents were making the news. The May 3, 1918, *Roundup Record* reported that a miner, Joe Stigler, of Carpenter Creek was almost tarred and feathered by a delegation of seventy-five "patriotic citizens" who were incensed that Stigler refused to aid the war effort and had opposed supporting the Red Cross. Although he had money in the bank, Stigler refused to buy Liberty Bonds or savings stamps. "It was first decided by the committee to tar and feather him—the necessary implements and materials being near at hand," the *Record* observed. "But on a motion to reconsider, he was ordered to leave camp."

SEDITION AND IMPEACHMENT

During the same February 1918 Extraordinary Session, the legislature passed the Montana Sedition Law. It basically outlawed any kind of utterance, written or verbal, critical of the U.S. government, the war, the draft, or the military. The punishment for an offense was not less than $200 and not more than $20,000, or imprisonment for not less than a year and not more than twenty.

Writing for the *Smithsonian* in 2015, Patrick Sauer noted that, under Montana's sedition law, "some 200 people in the state were arrested and 125 went to trial." Of those, 79 would be convicted and 41 sent to prison. The Montana law became the model for the federal Sedition Act, with only three words changed. Under the federal act, 2,000 people were arrested across the United States and some 900 imprisoned, none of them for espionage.

A number of newspapers in Montana perpetuated inflammatory coverage of alleged sedition that turned neighbor against neighbor. In March 1918, the *Roundup Record* reported that in Lewistown "an impromptu crowd called Edward Foster in and told him to kiss the flag." Foster, a Montana veteran of the Spanish-American War, was a prominent businessman. He was later arrested for allegedly uttering "seditious sentiments."

The *Record* article continued: "The crowd then went to the High School, secured all the German textbooks, carried them to the business center and burned them amid cheers and the singing of patriotic songs. Following this, ten more suspected pro-Germans were required to kiss the flag and to take an oath of allegiance." Later the crowd paraded through town, "headed by the Elks trumpet corps." Interestingly, just a few weeks later, in April, arsonists burned down the high school itself.

Amid such frenzy, furor, and hysteria, Felkner Haynes mounted his attack on Judge Crum. It would come at an extremely vulnerable time for Crum, during February and March 1918, when Crum's son Claude was

A crowd watches German textbooks burn in Lewistown on March 27, 1918. PHOTOGRAPH COURTESY OF THE LEWISTOWN PUBLIC LIBRARY.

hospitalized in Miles City with cancer. Because of his devotion to his son, he was not able to fully mount a defense of himself.

Crum was outspoken in his opposition of the war, particularly before the United States officially entered it. It may have been his tendency to expound and orate that alienated some neighbors. Many, however, seemed to excuse some of his "nonconformist views on the war" because they respected him. In Forsyth, the Presbyterian minister said, "[We] just threw the statements away with the remark that 'He has gone crazy on the subject' . . . that he talked himself into a state of mind on it where he simply could not help but talk about that."

After rumors circulated about him being pro-German, Crum stated during one of his court sessions in September 1917 that he was "strictly pro-American" and defended the Constitutional right of freedom of speech. However, this wouldn't satisfy Haynes and other "super patriots." Crum had thwarted Haynes at least three times: twice in court over legal opposition to Haynes' disregard for the Constitution and once in the culminating confrontation at the capitol when Crum drew his revolver in self-defense.

TWO COURT CASES

In September 1917, Crum released three Industrial Workers of the World (Wobblies) Haynes had arrested on suspicion of arson. Crum intervened when the Rosebud County sheriff took away their bedding and fed them only bread and water after they wrote Wobbly slogans on their cell walls. Crum ordered that the bedding be restored and that they be fed. He later released them from the Rosebud County Jail for lack of evidence.

Then in October 1917, Haynes had Rosebud County residents Ves Hall and A. J. Just arrested under the National Espionage Act because of statements they made about the war. He had them brought to Forsyth but had not yet jailed them while awaiting instructions from U.S. District Attorney Burton K. Wheeler in Butte. The pair sought out Crum for advice, who recommended they immediately head to Butte to talk with Wheeler. Haynes found out and wired the Butte sheriff, who arrested them when they stepped off the train. Haynes was incensed and vented his anger in a press statement that was a scarcely veiled attack on Crum: "We must be either Americans or anti-Americans." Haynes said there was no middle ground and that criticizing the government was to "sow the seeds of sedition."

Crum and Haynes again clashed on January 26, 1918, when Haynes assisted with prosecuting Hall before federal Judge George M. Bourquin in Helena, and Crum appeared as a character witness for Hall.

Bourquin acquitted Hall, ruling that although Hall had spoken out against the president and armed forces, he had not interfered with the military when doing so. It was following this trial that Haynes violently confronted Crum in the state capitol. As recounted by historian Walter, Crum later described the confrontation:

> **I started to leave the office, when I encountered Mr. Haynes . . . he became very angry and stated that there would be a killing in**

> **Rosebud County within a very short time over the Hall decision . . . he . . . advanced toward me, telling me that I was pro-German. When I saw that I was about to be assaulted, I took my small automatic from my overcoat pocket and told him to stop. I also told him that he was an infamous liar, a thief, a perjurer, and I used many other vile names.**

—~—

Within a few days, Forsyth's Committee of One Hundred, a self-appointed watchdog group, called a meeting and interrogated Crum for two hours. This group, and others like it, sprang up in Montana, according to Walter, to establish "local standards of Americanism." The ad hoc group had the endorsement of the Rosebud County Council of Defense. The committee accused Crum of "non-participation in the war movement" and demanded he resign his judgeship, which Crum refused to do. Instead, he immediately left for Miles City, where his son Claude was hospitalized with terminal cancer.

Meanwhile, "super patriots" were outraged that Hall was not convicted. Among them was *Helena Independent* editor Will Campbell, who wrote to Montana Senator Henry L. Myers demanding action and complaining of "the absolute inability to secure punishment for slackers or preachers of sedition. . . .", wrote Clemens P. Work in his book, *Darkest Before Dawn: Sedition and Free Speech in the American West.* Governor Stewart agreed and was ready to take action, calling a special Extraordinary Session of the legislature for February 14 to February 25, 1918.

Haynes secured fifteen affidavits alleging pro-German statements and actions by Crum that he delivered to Stewart on February 21, who forwarded them to the Montana Legislature, according to Walter. The House drafted articles of impeachment, and Crum was served the impeachment papers on February 28.

Crum, who was already under enormous stress from his son's illness, suffered a nervous breakdown and was on bed rest in Miles City. Three prominent attorneys came to his aid, and after consulting with other Montana attorneys and getting advice on the mood in the legislature, they advised Crum to resign if it would eliminate the planned impeachment hearing.

Governor Stewart agreed to this and accepted Crum's March 10 resignation, but then reneged on his promise.

In his resignation, Crum wrote, "A trial of my case would simply provide an opportunity for certain people to pose before the public and in the press as super patriots. It would give these people opportunities to color and distort statements I have made until they have no resemblance to the true facts." He added that it would be an opportunity for "personal enemies to spread venom and poison and pollute the atmosphere." His words couldn't have been more prescient. The three-day impeachment trial opened in the Senate on March 20 and proceeded without him there to defend himself, nor did he have any attorneys there on his behalf.

Despite a letter of support by eighty-five Roundup citizens, with several of them testifying in person on his behalf, the Senate impeached Crum on March 22, 1918, finding him guilty of all six articles of impeachment and removing him from the bench. He was also banned from ever holding public office in Montana. He was just forty-four years old.

Crum was found "guilty of high crimes and misdemeanors and malfeasance in office." The impeachment article specifications are a repetitious litany of his alleged statements opposing the United States going to war, that President Wilson was a tool of the British government and Wall Street, Crum's questioning the legal grounds for a military draft, and his predictions that people would riot against the draft. Other impeachment articles addressed his carrying a concealed weapon and pulling it on Haynes, his intervening on behalf of the Wobblies, and his advice to Just and Hall to flee Forsyth and talk to Wheeler. In the final article, Crum is accused of advising and counseling and abetting deeds that were "illegal and disloyal in their nature" and that gave "aid and comfort to the enemies of the United States in time of war."

During its February special session, the legislature had also threatened federal Judge George M. Bourquin (see Chapter 3), drafting a resolution calling for his resignation, which was tabled. Another resolution demanding Burton K. Wheeler's resignation failed by a 30 to 29 vote. Both Wheeler and Bourquin held federal offices, which the state legislature had no power over. But such was not the case with Crum.

The impeachment ruined Crum's life, not only in Montana in 1918, but later in North Dakota, where he tried to rebuild his life, law practice, and a new political career. In 1920, he was nominated for the State House from Oliver County in North Dakota by the Nonpartisan League. But then the American Legion Chapter in the town of Center circulated news about his impeachment, and he withdrew from the race.

On January 25, 1991—more than seven decades after his impeachment—a hearing was held before the Montana Senate Judiciary Committee to exonerate Crum. Historian Dave Walter testified that Crum "retreated to a low-profile, undistinguished law career in Mandan and Bismarck. He died in Kansas in 1948—a man whose spirit had been broken and whose life had been ruined by the Montana impeachment thirty years earlier." Two of Crum's grandchildren asked Walter to look into his impeachment and the possibility of his exoneration, prompting the hearing. It was something that Crum hoped and believed would happen some day.

In a final public statement in the *Forsyth Democrat* in 1919, Crum had said, "I have a sublime faith in the natural honesty and sense of justice of the American people, and feel sure that at some future time the right thinking people of the great State of Montana will undo the wrong that has been inflicted upon me, and that those who were responsible for my misfortune will be made to feel the justifiable wrath of a rational and humane sentiment." Sadly, Crum did not live to see his hopes fulfilled.

"In his final days, the judge was an alcoholic," testified his grandson Darwin Crum at the 1991 committee hearing. When his father had helped the judge into bed, he would say that the judge was sick. "I believe he was sick. I believe he was sick in heart and soul about a life destroyed. And a dream denied," said Darwin Crum.

On January 26, 1991, the Montana Senate exonerated Crum by a 46 to 0 vote. They also gave his grandchildren, who were sitting in the gallery, a standing ovation following the vote. In its deliberations, the Senate Judiciary Committee cited two legal grounds for the Senate's exoneration. Crum had already resigned his office and, therefore, under the terms of the 1889 Montana Constitution, he could not be impeached. The bill sponsor, Senator Harry Fritz, a Democrat from Missoula, further noted that Governor Stewart reneged on a promise that the impeachment proceeding would be dropped if Crum resigned. The Senate Judiciary Committee also found that Crum was denied the right to defense counsel, whereas all other impeachment trials in the nation had the best legal minds serving on the defense teams.

Montana would later right another historic wrong. In 2006, the state exonerated seventy-eight of those who had been convicted of sedition (one had already been pardoned). Fritz, who was also a history professor at the University of Montana, said, "It was a time of super-patriotic hysteria. It wouldn't have happened any other time."

Years ago, U.S. District Judge George M. Bourquin, rephrasing the words of George Bernard Shaw, said of that time: "During the war, the courts in France, bleeding under German guns, were very severe; the courts in England, hearing but the echoes of those guns, were grossly unjust; but the courts in the United States, knowing naught save censured news of those guns, were stark, staring, raving mad."

CHAPTER 3

Standing Up to Mass Hysteria and Mob Rule: *Maverick Judge George M. Bourquin*

Judge Charles L. Crum wasn't the only Montanan who refused to be cowed by mob mentality during World War I.

Furor over the judicial decisions of U.S. District Judge George M. Bourquin spurred calls for his removal from office, an aborted legislative vote to do just that, and a dangerously reactionary response to one of his rulings. Lawmakers in Montana were so incensed by one of his decisions that they passed one of the most repressive state laws ever put on the books, which resonated across the country.

EARLY LIFE

Bourquin was born June 24, 1863, near Tidioute, Pennsylvania. The son of a Swiss blacksmith and farmer, Justin Bourquin, and his French wife, Celestine (nee Ducray), George was the ninth of ten children and attended a one-room schoolhouse. Although he came from a seemingly humble background, he was descended from a long line of savvy individuals who had held important political and religious positions, according to Tel-Aviv University history professor and Bourquin's biographer, Arnon Gutfeld. "Research into the history of the family in Switzerland and in France . . . reveals that numerous ancestors were well educated," Gutfeld wrote. "Many of them were dissenters, iconoclasts, and opponents of authorities and consensus."

At age seventeen, George was asked to stay on and teach at his school, but a year later he headed west to join his brothers in Colorado, where he worked as a cowboy, miner, and smelterman. Arriving in Butte in June 1884, he worked in the silver mills and began reading law in 1889 in preparation for becoming an attorney. Five years later he was admitted to the Montana Bar. In 1904, he was elected district judge in Silver Bow County, and in 1912 was appointed U.S. district judge for Montana by President William H. Taft.

Although politically ambitious, Bourquin was by no means a stereotypical back-slapping, hand-shaking politician. According to Gutfeld, "He preferred an isolated life." As Gutfeld's research reveals, "contemporaries described Bourquin as vain, arrogant, and irascible yet merciful, fair, and just." He was also described as "austere and caustic tongued" and "handsome and distinguished looking." He was said to have "no intimate friends," preferring to keep others at a distance, lest they try to discuss pending cases. In fact, he was known to insist that empty chairs at his restaurant table be tilted forward so that people would be discouraged from sitting down and joining him.

Judge George Bourquin, shown here circa 1922, defended citizens' constitutional rights despite hysteria and hostility from so-called super patriots. PHOTOGRAPH COURTESY OF THE MONTANA HISTORICAL SOCIETY RESEARCH CENTER ARCHIVES.

As Gutfeld noted, "He was an imposing figure in both stature and personality. His oratorical prowess impressed all who heard him." His passion for the classics, history, and philosophy influenced the style and content of his thinking and legal writing.

Bourquin also had a passion for upholding the law. Even when he personally disagreed with the defendant's beliefs, he fiercely defended their rights. Gutfeld wrote, "In the face of great hostility and hysteria he often stood alone in defending legitimate dissent with which he disagreed."

According to Gutfeld, Bourquin's "most important and historically significant rulings occurred during the tumultuous days of World War I and the Red Scare that followed." He was, Gutfeld wrote, "one of the few judges who protected freedom of expression during times of crisis."

One such case was that of rancher Ves Hall. This was the same case that would lead to the demise of the career of Montana District Judge Charles L. Crum, who appeared as a character witness for Hall (see Chapter 2 on Judge Charles L. Crum).

A TIME OF PARANOIA

To put Bourquin's court decision regarding Ves Hall in perspective, it is important to understand just how toxic and paranoid the atmosphere in Montana was at the time.

In the years prior to World War I, many Montanans had been outspoken in opposing the nation's entry into the war enveloping Europe and were fearful of being dragged into it. But once the United States declared war on April 6, 1917, attitudes abruptly changed.

Rampant patriotism swept across Montana and the country. Espionage and sedition laws were quickly enacted and enforced. Citizens unleashed violence against both neighbors and strangers whom they considered disloyal. It went beyond mere accusations. There were lynchings, murders, beatings, public humiliations, and denunciations "of those," wrote Gutfeld, "who did not conform to 100 percent Americanism." Historian K. Ross Toole also documented the hysteria, reporting that "hundreds of suspects were hauled before Montana's Council of Defense to answer charges based on the rankest kind of rumor."

Vicious attacks focused on anyone who was not wholeheartedly enthusiastic about the war. Among those singled out were labor unions, German-Americans, Irish-Americans, and, as Gutfeld wrote, "other hyphenated Americans," as well as "foreign ideas and immigration in general."

"Before the war was over, hysteria had solidified into one of the most implacable attacks on civil liberties in the history of the country," wrote Toole. To oppose the war was to be considered a traitor, or worse.

In 1917 and 1918, super-patriotic zealots in Montana were apparently convinced that German spies were running loose in the state. Some individuals reported German planes flying over Helena and the Bitterroot Mountains. How these flew nearly 5,000 miles from Germany to Montana and why of all places they would target Montana defies rational thought and common sense. However, that didn't stop certain members of the press from fanning the hysteria. According to Gutfeld, the Helena *Independent* offered a $100 reward to anyone who "could find the airplane flying over the city." The paper's editor, Will Campbell, turned the *Independent* into a major mouthpiece for super-patriot conspiracy theories. Campbell penned an editorial to whip up hysteria, writing, "Are the Germans about to bomb the capital of Montana?" The paper would later boast that a "Helena citizen, unnamed, had fired the first shots in America at an airplane." Campbell, it should be noted, was also a fanatical member of the Montana Council of Defense (MCD).

Adding to this bizarre scenario was Montana Governor Sam V. Stewart promising "to follow the plane next time with an expert rifleman." Reportedly, there were also hundreds of rumors circulating about certain individuals being German spies and, as Gutfeld wrote, "mysterious cars with an even more 'mysterious wireless'" (meaning a radio).

VES HALL CASE

On January 26, 1918, the frenzy and paranoia came to a head in a Helena courtroom with Judge Bourquin presiding. This was less than a year after the United States' entry into the war.

Rosebud County rancher Ves Hall was arrested for uttering allegedly seditious remarks and charged under the National Espionage Act. District attorneys from all over the country had been using the Espionage Act to shut down free speech.

Gutfeld wrote that action could be taken against someone if they made "false statements" that were "intended to interfere with the operations or success of the armed forces or to promote insubordination within their ranks." The law also made it a federal crime to obstruct the recruitment and enlistment of men for service.

A summary of the trial transcript documented the allegations against Hall. Between July and October 1917, Hall reportedly stated that if the government wanted him to fight the Germans, they would have to kill him first, that Germany would beat the United States, that draftees were fools to go fight, and that Germany had the right to sink the *Lusitania* and kill Americans without warning. He allegedly called President Wilson a "British tool," "a Wall Street tool," "the richest man in the United States," and "the crookedest son of a bitch that ever sat in the President's chair."

Bourquin made a directed verdict acquitting Hall, which means Bourquin found the evidence flimsy and not sufficient to convict. Although Bourquin considered Hall's statements "unspeakable," the words didn't justify a guilty verdict of espionage. Bourquin hoped to set a precedent with this case and halt the misuse of the Espionage Act to stifle free speech.

He ruled that "Hall had made his statements in a small Montana town of sixty people, sixty miles from the nearest railroad," with "none of the armies or navies within hundreds of miles." Gutfeld described Bourquin's reasoning:

"Hall made them in a hotel kitchen, at a picnic, in the street, and in a 'hot and furious saloon argument.' Bourquin found no proof of intent to interfere with the military. He illustrated his decision with the statement that if [person] A shot [at person] B with a .22 pistol from a distance of three miles, A could not be convicted of attempted murder."

FALLOUT OF THE HALL DECISION

Apoplectic is one way to describe the Montana response to Bourquin's ruling. Fury and a huge outcry from politicians and the press over Bourquin's decision spurred Governor Stewart to immediately call a special session of the legislature. Will Campbell, the vitriolic editor of the *Helena Independent*, predicted bloodshed, writing, "Feeling is running high and I really expected some killing as a result of the construction of the law in the Hall case."

The MCD was initially set up at the urging of President Wilson, who hoped that state councils of defense could help boost food production and raise money for the war effort. In Montana, the MCD quickly set up county and community councils, which attracted "super patriots," who saw themselves as watchdogs of Americanism, reporting their neighbors as unpatriotic or suspicious, seeding paranoia, and holding inquisitions.

The paranoia gripping the state is evidenced in one of Campbell's hysterical headlines in the *Independent*, which screamed, **"Your Neighbor, Your Maid, Your Lawyer, Your Waiter May Be A German Spy."**

According to historian Dave Walter, "the hysteria finally played out" in the early 1920s, but some "hard-core purveyors of intolerance moved into the Montana realm of the Ku Klux Klan."

Although many at the time hated Bourquin's decision, his bravery and fairness in delivering it stands out decades later. K. Ross Toole wrote, "In retrospect,

The Helena Independent

HELENA, MONTANA, SUNDAY MORNING, MARCH 24, 1918.

Your Neighbor, Your Maid, Your Lawyer Your Waiter, May Be A German Spy

Will Campbell, managing editor of the Helena Independent, *used his newspaper to spread paranoia and fear.* PHOTOGRAPH COURTESY OF THE *HELENA INDEPENDENT.*

the Ves Hall decision was not only courageous, it was based on incontrovertible rectitude as far as law was concerned."

Despite the fact that it was the right decision, the backlash proved a victory for the super patriots. In his February 14, 1918, address to the legislative special session, Governor Stewart called "for action to enact a law here in Montana that will make available a mighty means of throttling the traitor and choking the traducer."

He told the lawmakers, "Every disloyal utterance and every treasonable act is duly reported to the German people. . . . The tender mother is startled by the mere suggestion that [her] boy may not come back, the father clenches his fists at the very suspicion that any of his own acquaintances might conspire to encompass the destruction of his son and heir."

Toole noted that "in the Annals of the State of the State Messages," which were typically pedestrian, "Stewart's address is remarkable for the high pitch of its frenzy and the admixture of tear-jerking sentimentality and violent references to 'traitors in our midst,' 'poisoned tentacles,' and 'vipers circulating the propaganda of the junkers.'"

By the end of the 1918 special session, lawmakers unanimously passed a repressive Sedition Act that would be a template for a federal act. The sedition law made it a crime to say or publish anything "disloyal, profane, violent, scurrilous, contemptuous or abusive" about the government, soldiers, or the American flag. The legislature unanimously passed the bill in February 1918, and Governor Stewart signed it into law.

The eventual result was that seventy-nine people in Montana were convicted under this law. Forty-one of them were imprisoned, serving sentences of one to twenty years and levied fines of $200 to $20,000, forever altering, and in some cases ruining, their lives.

The 1918 legislature also approved a Criminal Syndicalism Act, outlawing the Industrial Workers of the World (IWW) and gutting union organizing, and then they

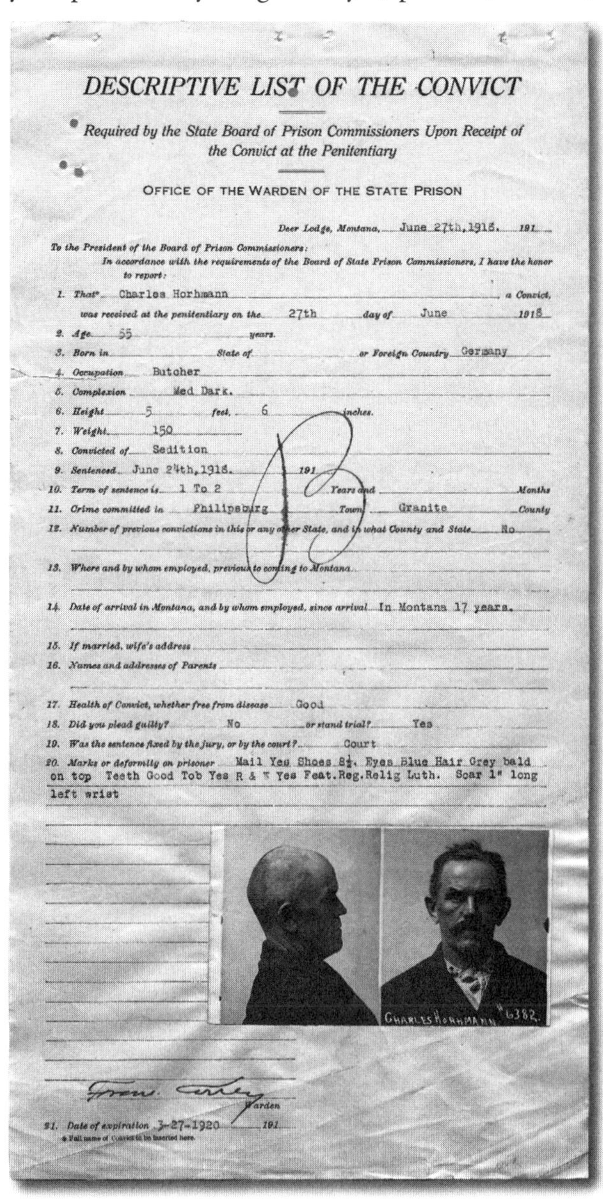

DESCRIPTIVE LIST OF THE CONVICT

Required by the State Board of Prison Commissioners Upon Receipt of the Convict at the Penitentiary

OFFICE OF THE WARDEN OF THE STATE PRISON

Deer Lodge, Montana, June 27th,1918. *191*

To the President of the Board of Prison Commissioners:

In accordance with the requirements of the Board of State Prison Commissioners, I have the honor to report:

1. *That** Charles Horhmann *a Convict, was received at the penitentiary on the* 27th *day of* June *1918*
2. *Age* 55 *years.*
3. *Born in* *State of* *or Foreign Country* Germany
4. *Occupation* Butcher
5. *Complexion* Med Dark.
6. *Height* 5 *feet,* 6 *inches.*
7. *Weight* 150
8. *Convicted of* Sedition
9. *Sentenced* June 24th,1918. *191*
10. *Term of sentence is* 1 To 2 *Years and* *Months*
11. *Crime committed in* Philipsburg *Town* Granite *County*
12. *Number of previous convictions in this or any other State, and in what County and State* No
13. *Where and by whom employed, previous to coming to Montana*
14. *Date of arrival in Montana, and by whom employed, since arrival* In Montana 17 years.
15. *If married, wife's address*
16. *Names and addresses of Parents*
17. *Health of Convict, whether free from disease* Good
18. *Did you plead guilty?* No *or stand trial?* Yes
19. *Was the sentence fixed by the jury, or by the court?* Court
20. *Marks or deformity on prisoner* Mail Yes Shoes 8½. Eyes Blue Hair Grey bald on top Teeth Good Tob Yes R & W Yes Feat.Reg.Relig Luth. Scar 1" long left wrist

Warden

21. *Date of expiration* 3-27-1920 *191*

* Full name of Convict to be inserted here.

Charles Horhmann of Philipsburg was convicted of sedition, sentenced on June 24, 1918, and sent to the state prison in Deer Lodge. PHOTOGRAPH COURTESY OF THE MONTANA STATE PRISON, MONTANA STATE HISTORICAL SOCIETY RESEARCH CENTER ARCHIVES.

Burton Kendall Wheeler, seen here circa 1922, openly criticized the Sedition Act of 1918. After World War I, Wheeler represented Montana as a U.S. senator from 1923 to 1947. PHOTOGRAPH COURTESY OF THE LIBRARY OF CONGRESS, LC-DIG-GGBAIN-35.

vindictively voted to serve Montana District Judge Charles Crum with articles of impeachment (see Chapter 2). Legislators also introduced joint resolutions calling for federal district attorney Burton K. Wheeler and Judge Bourquin to resign. The Wheeler resolution failed by one vote and the one regarding Bourquin was withdrawn, noted K. Ross Toole, because of "his reputation for dealing with any interference with the processes of his court through stiff contempt penalties."

These two bills, the Criminal Syndicalism Law and the Sedition Act, shut down virtually all opposition to the war. The laws "made it a penal offense for any person to write or speak against the war or conscription. They made no distinction between those who opposed the war on principle and those who actually threatened national security," according to Toole.

Montana journalism professor Clemens P. Work, author of *Darkest Before Dawn*, called the Montana Sedition Act "probably the harshest anti-speech law in the history of the country." Work also noted that, three months later, the U.S. Congress adopted Montana's sedition law, changing only three words.

Throughout his career Bourquin wasn't cowed by the MCD, super patriots, the federal government, or the powerful mining and lumber magnates of Montana. He continued in his career to take other unpopular stances, such as protecting the rights of union organizers, immigrants, and Native Americans.

BOURQUIN'S OTHER DECISIONS AND STANDS

Notably, Bourquin was an outspoken critic of rabid patriotism. In 1918, when influenza was gaining a toehold in the Big Sky, a Montanan, E. V. Starr, refused to kiss the flag, calling it "a piece of cotton" that could be covered in "microbes."

He had been sentenced to not less than ten and not more than twenty years of hard labor, as well as a $500 fine, according to Work. Bourquin stated that Starr was "more sinned against than sinner." He further said that the accused was "in the hands of those too common mobs, bent upon vindicating its peculiar standard of patriotism." Bourquin called kissing the flag "a spectacle for the pity as well as the laughter of gods and men." He considered the charge "frivolous," saying a small fine would have served justice. Although Bourquin believed he could not relieve Starr of his sentence, he urged him to appeal to pardoning authorities.

Bourquin also opposed deportations of radicals and dissenters, often locking horns with the government, wrote Gutfeld. In the case of the U.S. Department of Labor seeking to deport Nicholas Radivoeff, who was secretary of the Butte branch of the IWW, Bourquin found that the government had illegally seized pamphlets when it arrested Radivoeff, had not given him adequate time to hire an attorney, and that the department's proceedings had been unfair and prejudiced.

Bourquin particularly believed that deportation proceedings had to be fair and supported by substantial evidence. Anything less and the proceedings became "evil and dangerous" and risked undermining the nation's legal foundations. It was the role of the courts to ensure "public, humane, and just administration of the law."

In another deportation case involving an IWW member that Gutfeld recounted, John Jackson was accused of advocating for the destruction of property. Bourquin found in favor of the accused. He then found the state guilty of the crimes it had arrested Jackson for.

"There was no disorder save that of the raiders," Bourquin said, stating the arresting officers had "broke and destroyed property . . . arrested persons, seized papers and documents, cursed, insulted, beat . . . and bayoneted union members by order of the commanding officer." They had also entered Jackson's apartment, "insulted his wife, searched his person and effects, arrested him . . . and in general . . . perpetrated a reign of terror, violence, and crime against citizen and alien alike, and whose only offence seems to have been peaceable insistence upon and exercise of a clear legal right."

Bourquin also clashed with the Department of Labor over its attempted deportation in 1915 of a Chinese student, Tam Chung, who was allegedly working without a permit. Tam Chung was a seventeen-year-old man living with his uncle in Butte. He occasionally helped in the family restaurant in return for his food and lodging. The secretary of labor ordered his deportation for working without a permit.

Evidence was presented that Tam Chung was receiving daily tutoring and his teacher considered him a "diligent student of good behavior."

In his decision, Bourquin chastised the secretary of labor and referred to a congressional agreement with the Chinese government allowing Chinese students to study in the United States, saying that it was not up to the secretary of labor "to violate the national promise, repudiate the treaty, and convert it into a mere scrap of paper."

Bourquin found that a Chinese student who had lawfully entered the country could lawfully perform labor and did not require an immigration official to grant permission. He further provided a long list of precedents in support of his decision and concluded: "That[,] in the face thereof[,] like executive deportations continue, to put it mildly is amazing, though not incomprehensible to students of history. And how many poor and friendless Chinese, unable to contest executive orders in the courts, have been so deported in defiance of our treaty, is at least food for disquieting thought."

BOURQUIN GAINS NATIONAL ATTENTION

In the 1920s, Bourquin obtained laudatory and prominent news coverage when he served as a visiting judge in Seattle and San Francisco, primarily due to a huge backlog of Prohibition cases in those cities. He was praised for how quickly he dispatched them. It seems that correspondents were somewhat smitten with Bourquin's personality, of which reporter C. H. Bailey wrote, "He has plenty of it."

Bailey explained further that "Judge Bourquin is as human on the bench as he is off, and he tells the puzzled defendants who have gotten tangled up in the web of the law what it's all about. Every newspaper in San Francisco, for days past, has been quoting pithy paragraphs Judge Bourquin has delivered from the bench."

Bailey pointed out that Judge Bourquin would tell the accused why he or she was getting a particular sentence and then tailor his comments to what the defendant would understand, reserving Shakespeare and the ancient Greeks for those who would know what he was talking about. Bailey continued:

> **He became a lawyer and succeeded because he knew men. "Justice," the judge said, "is the greatest thing in the world to hold society together. More, it is the only thing in the world that can hold society together. I try to administer justice and . . . let the punishment fit the offense. If a man is punished, understands why he is punished and appreciates that he got the punishment that was coming to him, no more and no less, it's not going to embitter him. He'll still emerge from punishment a good [citizen]."**

You "can't help but like him," wrote Bailey. "Even the fellows he's sent to jail—and he's sent a lot in a week—like him and respect him. Pretty good recommendation for a judge at that."

He further described Bourquin as having white hair, being very soft-spoken, "a little above average height, erect and square shouldered. His face is deeply lined and his features are rugged. It is a face one doesn't forget right away." Bailey wrote. Bourquin was "a fine looking gentleman," who "doesn't care one bit whether people like his decisions or not." This trait impressed biographer Gutfeld as well, who called Bourquin "an exceptional federal judge . . . a unique, highly original, and important western judge."

Despite harsh criticism of Bourquin during World War I, many remembered him as Montana's finest judge. He died on November 15, 1958, in Pennsylvania at the age of ninety-five.

In a memorial tribute printed in the January 6, 1959, *Montana Standard*, U.S. District Judge W. D. Murray credited Bourquin with having left his mark on the history of Montana during his twenty-two-year career, adding "that he had done more than any other federal judge for the Montana district, the members of the bar, and especially for the public."

In a January 5, 1959, memorial written by twelve Montana attorneys and presented at a special ceremony in Butte federal court, they stated: "The lowliest man charged with offenses in Judge Bourquin's court was protected by him against any encroachment upon the rights accorded to the defendant by the law, either by his own counsel or opposing government lawyers."

As Gutfeld wrote, "The common theme of his legal thinking was to protect the individual from the excesses of governmental power."

Bourquin was also lauded in a 2006 letter to Governor Brian Schweitzer that asked for posthumous pardons for seventy-eight persons convicted of sedition in 1918 and 1919. (One of the seventy-nine convicted for sedition had been pardoned a year after the war ended.)

The letter's authors, University of Montana law professor Jeffrey Renz and journalism professor Clemens P. Work, wrote, "One of the nation's true judicial heroes of this era, federal District Court Judge George Bourquin of Montana, observed at the time that the prosecution of such individuals betrayed both 'the genius of democracy and spirit of our people.' Judge Bourquin's views later became the law of the United States." ⸻

CHAPTER 4

Almost Lynched: Glendive Minister John M. Franz

—*The Persecution of Conscientious Objectors*

On a windy Saturday in April 1918, Mennonite minister John M. Franz stood beneath a towering poplar in a badlands canyon outside Glendive, a noose around his neck. He was surrounded by a self-appointed "jury" of twelve men that included Dawson County Sheriff George Twible. They had decided, without formal charges or a trial, to deliver Franz to their own kind of justice.

His crime? Franz was a conscientious objector. And he spoke German. He also aided Mennonite farmers seeking draft furloughs and deferments. These facts made him the focus of hostile suspicion during this volatile, "super-patriotic" time in Montana during World War I.

Franz and other members of the Bethlehem Mennonite Church opposed the war and refused to support it in any way. Mennonites, like Hutterites and Amish, are faith-based pacifists who embrace nonresistance and nonviolence. Just a year earlier, the Mennonites' opposition to the war was little different from that of their Glendive neighbors. That is, until the United States was reluctantly pushed to enter the Great War after a series of German provocations, including the sinking of American and British ships and an attempt by Germany to turn Mexico against the United States. Prior to that time, opposition to American involvement was widespread. But suddenly, those opposing

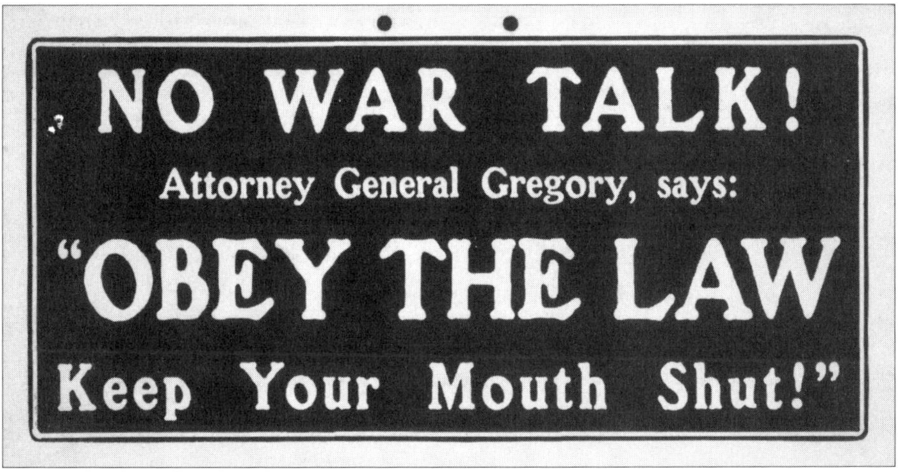

With anti-German fever running high, government officials—like U.S. Attorney General Thomas Gregory—often trampled on basic constitutional rights. PHOTOGRAPH COURTESY OF THE LIBRARY OF CONGRESS, LC-USZC4-9013.

the war, and particularly those who spoke German or had any ancestral connection to Germany, were eyed by their neighbors with suspicion as possible traitors and spies. This was true even in the somewhat isolated Bloomfield Settlement, the home of Franz's church. The prosperous agricultural area was about forty miles north of Glendive, the Dawson County seat.

But no corner of the state was left untouched by the war. Nearly 40,000 Montanans served, which meant almost 10 percent of the population went to war. Historian Michael P. Malone, in *Montana, A History of Two Centuries*, writes that Montana sent a higher percent of its men to war than any other state, "a rate of contribution that exceeded that of the next highest state by 25 percent. Montanans also suffered a record percentage of casualties—939 Montanans died."

Although Franz was an American citizen born in Minnesota, he spoke and read German. And for this particular group of men in the lynching party, that was evidence enough. That fateful afternoon, Franz stood with an iron-hand grip on the noose to prevent it from tightening around his neck and calmly reasoned with the vigilantes, asking to be taken to Glendive for a courtroom trial.

"You, Mr. [Twible], are the sheriff of this county," Franz said, according to an article written for *Mennonite Life* in 1952 by his oldest son, Rufus. "I voted for you because I believed in you and trusted you. You were to give me protection if and when I should need it. Now you are not giving me that protection."

Also in the circle of angry men were two prominent local attorneys, a banker, and several businessmen and cattlemen. Franz addressed one of the attorneys, who remained unnamed in the article but who presumably held an elected position based on Rufus' account. "You are the attorney representing the law and representing us before the law," Franz said. "I too, gave assent to your position and now you, too, are opposing me by this method. I am wondering why you are doing this. Could you not give me a hearing on this matter?"

As a last resort, Franz said to the sheriff, George Twible, "You don't want a record of this hanging going down in the history of this county, do you?" Twible began to listen to Franz and urged the other men to do so, too.

Just a few hours earlier, Franz had been on his farm, hitching his horses to the family buggy. He had set out with his pregnant wife, Regina, and their two young sons, Rufus and Ewald, for a nearby school meeting. When they arrived at the school, "We noticed a number of strangers, two carloads of them," recalled Rufus.

As Regina and the boys entered the school building, Franz went to get his mail from his mailbox across from the school. Among the items were his hometown newspaper, the *Mountain Lake Observer*, which contained several pages of German news about local affairs in Mountain Lake, Minnesota.

Shortly after the school meeting began, a man came in and asked Franz to step outside. Franz left, taking his mail with him. He was immediately accosted by several men who forced him toward one of the cars. When Franz asked why they were taking him, they said he was in possession of a German newspaper. According to Rufus, "They threatened 'to fix him' giving as their reason that he was the leader of the Germans in this settlement, meaning the Mennonites."

Franz asked to see his wife, but was told this wasn't necessary. But Regina and some of the people at the school meeting had become suspicious that something was going on. She left the school building, approached the car, and asked the men what they were doing. She was told that it was "none of her business and that they were taking Father for a ride," recounted Rufus.

"She insisted that she go along and climbed on the running board of the car," and she saw guns, shovels, and a rope inside the car, Rufus wrote. John Franz had also noticed these items when he was forced into the car. One of the men—all of whom had been drinking alcohol—threw Regina forcibly to the ground although she was visibly pregnant at the time and would give birth to the Franzes' third son in two months.

The men quickly drove away, recounted Rufus, and took his father "to an isolated spot about thirty miles away in the Bad Lands [*sic*] of Montana where there was a large tree."

After John Franz reasoned with his accusers, Sheriff Twible changed his mind and persuaded the group of men to take Franz to the jail in Glendive.

As Rufus recounted, "We later discovered that the men agreed among themselves to hang father from a bridge over the Yellowstone River, probably with a greater number of people or a mob so they could do away with him later that evening." Meanwhile, Regina, after meeting with five church elders, headed into Glendive with them and went to the jail. Her repeated knocks on the jail door were ignored, until a jailer eventually answered and brusquely asked, "What do you want, lady?"

When she asked to see the sheriff, the jailer told her the sheriff wasn't there and he didn't know when he would be back. A few moments later, however, the sheriff stepped out a side door and told her and the Franz children that they could come back in a half hour and see John. At this point, Regina almost fainted in relief because she had feared her husband had already been killed.

The family reunited later that day, and Rufus later wrote, "I will never forget how my father looked at that moment. It seemed as though he had aged tremendously." John Franz was thirty-three years old at the time of his near lynching. His ordeal was not yet over, however. He was held in the jail over the weekend, but the sheriff allowed Regina and the children to stay with him.

At 7 p.m. on Monday, a crowd of about 200 people gathered at city hall. The minister was taken there for "what is commonly called a 'gorilla hearing,'" wrote Rufus. They put him in the center of the room and the others gathered around him. Members of the crowd began to fire questions at him.

"Are you a citizen?"

"Isn't it true you speak German?"

"The main charges centered about the idea that they thought he was 'pro German,'" recounted Rufus. They asked about his newspaper, and Franz explained it was his hometown newspaper and offered to translate every sentence, saying the German articles were local news that had nothing to do with Germany. Then they wanted to know why he and the other Mennonites refused to buy war bonds. Franz explained that the Mennonites supported the Red Cross, but that they were opposed to all war and therefore did not buy war bonds.

At the close of this so-called "hearing," the crowd decided to ban all German church services. They also placed John Franz under a $3,000 bond and ordered him to report to the district court four times a year until the close of the war. If no charges occurred during that time, the case would be dismissed. After Franz's first court appearance, however, his bond was cancelled. He was released from appearing in court again, and the case was dismissed.

Franz was lucky his accusers backed down, given that anti-German fervor was at a fever pitch in Montana. Perhaps some of them felt shame.

In his book, *More Montana Campfire Tales*, historian Dave Walter devoted a chapter to this disturbing period in Montana's history, titling it "Patriots Gone Berserk: The Montana Council of Defense, 1917–1918." He describes a climate of fear and paranoia. Teaching of the German language was banned in public and private schools. Anti-German fanatics drove the last German language newspaper, *Montana Staats-Zeitung*, out of business. And German was banned from church pulpits, which, as Walter wrote, "devastated a number of German language congregations in eastern Montana, particularly Lutheran, Congregational, Mennonite, and Hutterite groups."

Ministers wrote "heart-wrenching" letters to the Montana Council of Defense (MCD) pleading to use at least some German in communion and funeral services, since older members of the congregation didn't understand English. The MCD refused to change its Order #3, instead making it even more restrictive by banning church services in homes.

And as outrageous as it might seem, the near-lynching of a German-speaking minister was not inconceivable. On August 1, 1917, a fiery labor organizer for the Industrial Workers of the World (IWW) and anti-war activist, Frank Little, was hanged from a railroad trestle on the outskirts of Butte. Labor unions were particular targets of the super patriots, who gravitated to local councils of the MCD, and of American industry leaders, who used the war as an excuse to dismiss workers' demands.

In the case of Little's murder, it is widely suspected that the Anaconda Copper Mining Company may have been involved. It was actively engaged in accusing union miners of treason. The company's attacks on IWW members were ruthless and relentless. The Anaconda Company and industry leaders also demonized members of the left-wing Nonpartisan League (NPL), which was organizing farmers to fight high grain elevator fees, railroad shipping charges, and unfair taxes. An NPL organizer was brutally beaten in Miles City by members of a local "Third Degree Committee," according to Walter.

Not only were these attacks against workers and farmers cloaked in words of super patriotism, but, it seems, the attack on Franz and his Mennonite community may have been inspired by greed as well. It was later revealed that some families living near the Mennonites had spread misinformation about them, hoping to gain from the Mennonites' loss. Instead, locals (though not the Mennonites themselves) ran the fearmongers out of town.

Several prominent attorneys offered to sue for damages, wrote Rufus, but his father always declined, saying the case had been "left entirely in the hands of the Lord."

Sometime later, as John and Rufus worked in one of their fields, a man stopped his vehicle and walked across the field to talk to Franz, who immediately recognized him as one of the twelve men.

The attorney, F. S. P. Foss, apologized and asked Franz's forgiveness. Foss had been the youngest of the vigilante group and would go on to become the district judge for Dawson County. Franz offered forgiveness willingly, wrote his son, and later shared the apology with his church, which rejoiced at the news.

Foss offered to do legal work for Franz and to provide legal advice, should Franz ever need it. The other eleven men never apologized, wrote Rufus.

Elsewhere in Montana and across the country, Mennonites, Hutterites, Amish, and other conscientious objectors faced threats and abuse for their antiwar beliefs and German heritage. In some cases, people were killed because their behavior was deemed un-American.

World War I was one of the deadliest wars in human history, with an estimated 9 million fatalities among military combatants and as many as 13 million civilians killed from 1914 to 1918. Of the 4.7 million men who served in the U.S. armed forces, more than 116,000 died and another 200,000 were wounded. Many more suffered accidents, infections, and illness.

With so much at stake, emotions ran high among the citizenry back home. In his book about the persecution of Hutterites during WWI, *Pacifists in Chains,* Goshen College professor Duane C. S. Stoltzfus wrote that a "hyper-patriotic fever swept across the land, turning neighbor against neighbor in a relentless search for traitors. When these neighbors formed mobs, they set about their business with hanging rope, whip, tar and feathers, yellow paint, and midnight fires."

Stoltzfus' research focused primarily on the plight of Hutterite conscientious objectors in South Dakota who lived in sixteen communities, or colonies.

Sheriff's Proclamation

TO FOREIGN-BORN RESIDENTS

"I, S. W. Matlock, Sheriff of Yellowstone County, Montana, deem it wise in the present crisis, in this formal proclamation to assure all residents of foreign birth that although the United States has become actively involved in the great European war, no citizen of any foreign power, resident in the County of Yellowstone, State of Montana, need fear any invasion of his personal or property rights so long as he goes peaceably about his business and conducts himself in a law-abiding manner.

"The United States has never, in any war, confiscated the property of any foreign resident unless by his own hostile acts he made it necessary.

"I take this formal means of declaring to all foreign-born residents that they will be protected in the ownership of their property and money and that they will be free from personal molestation, so long as they obey the laws of the State and Nation and the ordinances of the City.

"I urgently request that all our people refrain from public discussion of questions involved in the present crisis and maintain a calm and considerate attitude toward all without regard to their nationality."

Let it be understood that every citizen owes undivided allegiance to the American flag, that he is expected to loyally fulfill all obligations which citizenship and residence impose upon him, and that any act, however slight, tending to give aid or comfort to the enemy is treason, for which severe penalties are provided in addition to that punishment which public opinion inflicts upon the memory of all traitors in all lands.

Dated at Billings, Montana, this 16th day of April, A. D. 1917.

S. W. Matlock,

Sheriff of Yellowstone County, Montana

In an April 16, 1917, proclamation, Yellowstone County Sheriff S. W. Matlock sought to assuage immigrants' fears and urge citizens to remain "calm and considerate" toward one another.
PHOTOGRAPH COURTESY OF THE BILLINGS HISTORIC DOCUMENT COLLECTION.

Their appearance—clothing, haircuts, beards—and lifestyle drew their neighbors' attention, and the fact that they spoke a Germanic language raised suspicions.

Stoltzfus noted that President Woodrow Wilson "warned that conformity would become a virtue and dissent a vice" once the United States entered the war. For conscientious objectors, Wilson's words could not have been more ominous. Indeed, people whose behavior was deemed nonconformist by their neighbors would find themselves on the receiving end of violent attacks.

Stoltzfus recounted incidents in McPherson County, Kansas, where Mennonite farmers—conscientious objectors based on their faith—refused to buy war bonds. In response, vigilantes whipped and tarred and feathered the farmers and vandalized their farms and property. In Fairview, Michigan, super patriots torched the Mennonite church. The crime was never investigated or prosecuted.

For some conscientious objectors of draft age, their beliefs would be not only dangerous, but fatal.

HUTTERITE BROTHERS "MARTYRED"

In *Pacifists in Chains,* Stoltzfus relates the tragic story of four young Hutterite farmers from South Dakota. They had been conscripted against their will and sent to Camp Lewis, a training camp for infantrymen in Washington State in July 1918. There they refused to perform any duties, including washing dishes, because they believed such labors would aid soldiers and thus the war effort.

Three of the farmers were brothers—Michael, David, and Joseph Hofer—and the fourth was their brother-in-law Jacob Wipf. All were from the Rockport Colony in South Dakota. When other soldiers at Camp Lewis filled out their induction forms and put on military uniforms, the four farmers refused. As a result, they were considered military prisoners subject to military law. They spent their first night at Camp Lewis in the guardhouse, where they remained for two months until they were court-martialed and sent to the federal penitentiary on Alcatraz Island. Each was sentenced to twenty years of hard labor.

David Hofer wrote home in August, "We all do not expect to see each other in this world anymore." Joseph also wrote home, saying, "It is very clear that we are not destined for better days ahead and that our lives will endure for only a short while."

At Alcatraz, the men were hung on chains by their wrists with their feet barely touching the cold, wet floor, "a technique," wrote Stoltzfus, "known as 'high cuffing,' well established in the history of torture." Their diet was bread and water. Guards provided them with military uniforms, which they refused to wear, instead remaining in their underwear. They lived in a "dank, windowless" basement day and night. Rats were their only company.

In November 1918, they were shipped to the military prison at Fort Leavenworth, Kansas. Two of the brothers would die while in custody: Joseph, twenty-four, on November 29 and Michael, twenty-five, a few days later. Their grave markers in South Dakota identify them as "martyrs." The official cause of death listed was "pneumonia," which was commonly the designation for those dying of influenza, wrote Stoltzfus. The third brother, David, was released at the time of their deaths, while Wipf was set free on April 13, 1919, eleven months after his arrest.

According to Stoltzfus, "the Hutterite church was convinced that the men died because of the manner in which they had been imprisoned in the weeks and months leading up to death. The official church history, the *Chronicle of the Hutterian Brethren*, states that Michael and Joseph Hofer 'died in prison as a result of cruel mistreatment by the United States military.'" This view was shared by The National Civil Liberties Bureau (later renamed the American Civil Liberties Union), which accused the government of torturing the four Hutterites.

Mennonite historian C. Henry Smith similarly concluded that the Hofer brothers "died as a result of exposure and torture received at the hands of prison guards." Stoltzfus said that another researcher, Darius Rejali, an expert in the history of torture (and author of *Torture and Democracy*), "concluded that the harshest prisoner punishments during the war fell on conscientious objectors like the Hutterites."

The four Rockport Hutterites were among 504 conscientious objectors court-martialed during the war. Of those, about 142 were Mennonite, Amish, or Hutterite. While the faiths of some conscientious objectors allowed them to take part in the Medical Corps or do other noncombatant work, that wasn't the case for the Hutterites, who were absolutist conscientious objectors. The four Hutterites testified that the only labor they could do was to work on a farm that would feed the needy and poor, but not soldiers.

At the beginning of U.S. entry in the war, there were eighteen Hutterite colonies in the country—two in Montana and sixteen in South Dakota. By the end of the war, only seven remained. The rest had moved en masse to Canada. Dave Walter's research shows that, in Montana, 700 Mennonite families that had settled in the Fort Peck and Chinook areas relocated to British Columbia in 1918.

The death and harassment of Hutterites for their pacifist views is not only tragic but ironic, considering that their pacifism is one of the reasons they were urged to migrate to the United States fifty years earlier. In the 1870s, President Ulysses S. Grant personally invited Hutterites in Russia to move to the United States, welcoming both "their farming skills and pacifist convictions," according to Stoltzfus. Emigration enabled the Hutterites to avoid conscription into the Russian army, but their pacifism fell under a different lens when the United States entered into World War I.

Later, during World War II, the United States demonstrated that it had learned from its painful history of mistreatment of conscientious objectors. The draft measure approved by Congress allowed conscientious objectors to be assigned to the Civilian Public Service to do "work of national importance" in lieu of military service.

During World War I, a group of military veterans went to the White House, asking President Wilson to release conscientious objectors held in federal prisons. PHOTOGRAPH COURTESY OF THE LIBRARY OF CONGRESS, LC-USZ62-39524.

CHAPTER 5

'Designed for Strife': Suffragist Hazel Hunkins

A brief biography of Hazel Hunkins could be bookended by two events: chaining herself to the front gates at the White House in 1917 and then sixty years later, in 1977, being honored in the Rose Garden by President Jimmy Carter for her tireless efforts to support women's rights.

At the time she met President Carter in 1977, she was believed to be one of the last living suffragists. She told him, "I don't know if I'm the last—but if I'm not the last, I'm certainly the noisiest."

Despite all the "noise" she made, most Montanans knew very little about Hunkins and her radical political activities until fairly recently. Montana historian, archaeologist, and cultural anthropologist Kevin Kooistra says that could be due to the fact that a lot of her actions and notoriety were downplayed in her hometown Billings newspaper.

But she got plenty of national coverage, often on the front page of major national newspapers, which seemed quite eager to photograph and interview her.

The writer of the July 8, 1917, *Houston Post*'s column, "Early Morning Observations," was presumably triggered by one of Hazel's more publicized actions when he wrote, "If we had known ten years ago that there was any such person as Miss Hazel Hunkins, we would have predicted then and there that she would make trouble. Prenominally and surnominally, Hazel Hunkins was designed for strife."

Hunkins, one imagines, probably chuckled with delight at her notoriety. She would dedicate most of her life to women's suffrage and women's rights and never backed down from challenging unjust laws. Ironically, she had wanted a much quieter life. In her youth, she had really wanted to be a chemist—a career path denied her only because she was a woman.

AN UNLIKELY PATH TO RABBLE ROUSER

Born in Aspen, Colorado, in 1890, Hazel moved to Billings in 1903 as a teenager. The daughter of E. Lewis Hunkins and Anna Whittingham Hunkins, who owned Hunkins Jewelers in downtown Billings, she attended Billings High School and excelled academically. Completing her high school studies in three years, she was the 1908 class valedictorian.

Pictures of her in the high school yearbook, the *Kyote Annual*, show her to be the only woman on the debating team, along with three male classmates. She was also a member of the women's basketball team.

But perhaps there is an inkling of the idealist she was. The *Billings Gazette* noted that Hunkins presented a speech by Jean Valjean from *Les Misérables*, winning a preliminary declamation contest during her senior year and going on to compete in Missoula at the State Declamation Contest.

In her brief three-year high school career, Hunkins racked up a trifecta of accomplishments in addition to being valedictorian—voted by her classmates as most popular, second smartest, and third most conceited.

She attended a year of college preparatory classes at Mount Ida School in Newton, Massachusetts, before attending Vassar College, earning a chemistry degree in 1913. She then worked toward a master's degree and taught in the chemistry department at the University of Missouri.

Returning home to Billings in 1916 to care for her ailing mother, Hazel taught at Billings High School. After her mother recovered, Hazel began applying for chemistry lab jobs but was repeatedly turned down. She was told several times that, although she was qualified, they didn't want a woman working in their labs. It was during this time that she became head of the newly formed local chapter of the Congressional Union for Woman Suffrage (CU).

By 1916, only eleven states and the Territory of Alaska had given women the right to vote, among them Montana. Alice Paul, leader of CU (which later became the National Woman's Party), believed progress was too slow and instead pushed for a constitutional amendment giving women throughout the United States the right to vote. Under Paul's leadership, the CU would become known as the militant branch of the National American Suffrage Association, borrowing tactics used by British suffragettes. Paul recruited Hunkins to join the cause—to campaign for the vote and to oppose President Woodrow Wilson, who was running for reelection.

Hunkins wasted no time. By September 26, 1916, her name appeared in a small article on the front page of the *Santa Ana Register*, identifying her as a lecturer for the National Woman's Party (NWP). According to the article, she flew over Redwood City, California, in an airplane, "showering party literature upon the townspeople." She would campaign for three years for the NWP, assisting state organizations and serving as organization secretary.

Around the world, women had been lobbying for the right to vote since at least the early 1800s, but it wasn't until the turn of the century that the movement began to gather steam. New Zealand led the way, with its parliament ratifying legislation admitting women to the ballot box in 1893. Other countries followed, with women's suffrage gaining approval in Australia in 1902, Finland in 1906, Norway in 1913, and Denmark and Iceland in 1915. In the United States, suffragists kept an eye on similar campaigns in Canada, Russia, Poland, Germany, and Great Britain.

Carrying the Stars and Stripes, Hazel Hunkins leads a line of suffragists heading to the White House to picket on February 14, 1917. PHOTOGRAPH COURTESY OF THE LIBRARY OF CONGRESS, MNWP-160-160018U.

SILENT SENTINELS PICKET WHITE HOUSE

Because of her passionate convictions, Hunkins was among the first women to volunteer with the "Silent Sentinels," a group of suffragists who, beginning in January 1917, stood in silence while picketing outside the White House with the intent of challenging and embarrassing Wilson to support the suffrage amendment.

They carried banners that read, "Mr. President How Long Must Women Wait For Liberty," and they unfurled a huge banner in front of the White House stating, "President Wilson is Deceiving the World When He Appears as the

Prophet of Democracy. President Wilson Has Opposed Those Who Demand Democracy for This Country. He's Responsible for the Disenfranchisement of Millions of Americans. We in America Know This. The World Will Find Him Out."

Years later, she would describe the picketing experience as "hell." Not only would they stand shivering in snow and rain and later in blistering heat, but they faced rude and abusive treatment at times, particularly after Congress declared war on Germany in April 1917. Some accused the suffragists of being unpatriotic and traitors, and attacked them both verbally and physically.

In a 1977 *Chicago Tribune* interview, Hunkins recalled being clubbed by police and pelted with eggs by a crowd when she spoke in Lafayette Square across from the White House.

In a 1980 *San Francisco Chronicle* article, she recalled, "The crowds were very unfriendly. We used to grit our teeth for the insults when the civil servants came out of work at 4 P.M. 'Dirty bitches—what are you doing here?' they would shout. Sometimes it was even worse than that."

Then, in late June 1917, Hunkins was among six suffragists arrested for trying to carry "militant" suffragist banners to the White House gates. Eleven more were detained on July 4. Ten days later, a third group was taken into custody. All the women were charged with "obstructing traffic."

Hazel Hunkins is bundled against the cold while picketing the White House during the winter in 1917. PHOTOGRAPH COURTESY OF THE LIBRARY OF CONGRESS, MNWP-152-152010U.

"The protesters were sentenced to sixty days in the workhouse. There, they suffered beatings, forced feeding, and unsanitary conditions," according to an article on the *American Experience* PBS documentary, "Wilson and Women's Suffrage." "But the pickets—and the arrests—continued. In August, scuffles broke out right in front of the White House gates. For three days suffragists were dragged, punched, and choked by angry crowds. City police stood by, refusing to intervene."

In a March 30, 1917, letter to her mother, Hunkins wrote of the picketing, "Oh, how I hate it," but added that it was working. "It is a wonderful piece of publicity. It got the message of the federal amendment across, the way nothing else has for ages—since Susan B. Anthony was stoned for a similar offence."

In the same letter, Hunkins wrote that she had been lobbying a lot, and she revealed her outrage at the status quo:

> **Can you imagine men still saying that women don't need the vote: that they are represented by the men: that man is naturely [*sic*] woman's superior: that women should wait til after the war: . . . . I never knew what made women bitter until I came here and saw the dominion men have over women and the way they lord it over them. If they are cornered in any way, they revert to the animal and insult her. . . . [I]f there is anything that can make me boil it is to be told by some great big fat pompous slobby dirty dishonest politician that women aren't capable of voting correctly and in the same breath say with a smirk that he'd do anything for the ladies. And to think that he has the power to decide on this question!**

Hazel would make the front page in a number of newspapers across the country when she was accosted in June 1917 by a woman in the mob outside the White House, a Mrs. Richardson of Missouri, who shouted, "You are a dirty, yellow traitor" as she grabbed for Hunkins' banner.

News reports said that Richardson physically attacked Hunkins and tore her clothing, while Hunkins scrambled up part of the fence to protect her banner. In a July 8, 1917, letter to her mother, Hunkins describes holding a banner that stated, "We demand democracy and self government in our own land." She went on, describing what happened next:

> **A Mrs. Richardson came up to me and said I ought to be ashamed of myself to stand there and hold that banner. [A short time later, Richardson] returned and took a hold of my banner and spit on it. My heart sank. It was the first time I had seen such venom and I only could meet it by absolutely ignoring it and saying nothing. . . . This woman then began to upbraid [me] for standing there when there was a war on and called me a traitor.**

Hunkins wrote that she handed her banner to a neighboring picketer for safekeeping and clasped Richardson's hands when she tried to attack her. A man snatched the banner and threw it into the crowd. "Well, anyway it was 'an Experience.' I never want to go through it again and I hate to read the accounts of it . . . but I cheer up and think . . . it will be funny stuff for my grandchildren to read."

Hunkins and her fellow picketers faced more than the wrath of Mrs. Richardson and the mob. Suffrage leaders, such as Carrie Chapman Catt, denounced them in public statements to the press, stating that suffragists should quit their protests because "picketing is harmful to the suffrage movement." There were also organizations of women who opposed women's suffrage, such as the Montana Association Opposed to Woman Suffrage.

"What was militant about the NWP was that no group had ever picketed the White House before," said Jennifer Krafchik, executive director of the Belmont-Paul Women's Equality National Monument, in an interview with *Washington Post* reporter Terence McCardle. "They used Wilson's words against him in their banners. Nobody had ever seen this before especially in a group of women. They were much more aggressive than any other suffragette group."

There was no shortage of ridicule in a number of newspapers, such as this condescending item in the *Helena Independent* in June 1917:

> **Hazel is simply one of the misguided 'friends' of the suffrage cause—she is part of the lunatic fringe which hangs forever around the edge of the suffrage cause. . . . Little Hazel Hunkins of Montana has been misled. It is the duty of Congresswoman Jeannette Rankin to hunt up the little Vassar graduate and pin a tag to her so she will not get lost on the long journey, then send her back to Montana. If Hazel is naughty when she gets out here in the sunshine where straight thinking is the rule, her mother should take her out behind the wood shed and let the neighbors hear the gentle patter of her slipper on the bustle of Hazel's overalls (We guess Suffragettes wear overalls).**

But all was not ridicule, and abuse, and arrests. In fact, Hunkins wrote her mother that parents were bringing their children to come by and see the demonstrators. In a July 5, 1917, letter to her mother, she wrote, "I have watched public opinion change in such a short time that I wouldn't be surprised to be greeted as a hero rather than as an offender sooner or later. A man came down the picket line the other day and said to me, 'I brought my little boy especially to see you girls. I wanted him to see history in the making.'" A photograph from this time shows her outside the White House gates smiling at a young girl who is presenting her with a large bouquet of roses.

In 1917, she left her paid position with NWP to work for the National War Labor Board as a researcher and occasional union investigator, according to a biographical piece written by staff at the Radcliffe Institute's Schlesinger Library, but Hunkins continued to participate in pickets. It was during this time she was arrested and sentenced to the Occoquan Workhouse (about

A young girl presents flowers to Hazel Hunkins outside the White House gates. PHOTOGRAPH COURTESY OF THE LIBRARY OF CONGRESS, MNWP.160019.

twenty miles outside of Washington, D.C.), where she participated in a hunger strike. The arrested women suffered such a notable level of abuse that they dubbed the incident "The Night of Terror," which was widely publicized by the press and galvanized the public.

In a retrospective on the centennial of The Night of Terror, veteran *Washington Post* reporter Terence McArdle set the scene. On October 20, 1917, Alice Paul was arrested while picketing the White House. She carried a banner that read, "The Time Has Come to Conquer or Submit. For Us, There is But One Choice. We Have Made It." These were President Wilson's own words that he used on posters supporting the war effort. Paul co-opted the president's battle cry, later explaining, "When men are denied justice, they go to war. This is our war, only we are fighting it with banners instead of guns."

Paul was taken to the Washington, D.C., jail, where she went on a hunger strike. "Doctors force-fed her twice a day with a tube down her throat—a process that caused her to vomit repeatedly," wrote McArdle. "William Alanson White, the superintendent of St. Elizabeth's Hospital, interviewed her in a vain attempt to have her committed. White found Paul to be sane and 'perfectly calm, yet determined.'"

Less than a month after Paul's arrest, Hunkins and other picketing suffragists were also arrested and sent to Occoquan. They demanded to be treated as political prisoners, but the prison superintendent told his guards to teach the women a lesson. History writer Sarah Pruitt paints a grim picture of their treatment. "[T]he guards dragged the women down the hall and threw them into dark, filthy cells," she writes.

> **[Lucy] Burns' had her hands shackled to the top of a cell, forcing her to stand all night; the guards also threatened her with a straitjacket and a buckle gag. Day (the future founder of the Catholic Worker Movement) was slammed down on the arm of an iron bench twice. Dora Lewis lost consciousness after her head was smashed into an iron bed; Alice Cosu, seeing Lewis' assault, suffered a heart attack, and didn't get medical attention until the following morning.**

The *Washington Post* and other newspapers covered the harsh treatment of the suffragists and it became a national embarrassment. Public opinion shifted in their favor. In March 1918, the Washington, D.C., court of appeals ruled that all the suffragist arrests were unconstitutional.

Protests continued, however, as did arrests. In an August 17, 1918, article, "60 Suffragists Under Arrest in U.S. Capitol," the Harrisburg [Pennsylvania] *Telegraph* reported, "Hazel Hunkins of Montana, carrying an American flag, led the group of women who were all dressed in white, bearing purple, white and gold banners of the woman's party. The banners demanded the President and his party stop obstructing suffrage in the Senate. They accused him of being in line with the Prussian Reichstag in denying them democracy."

Hunkins attempted to speak three times, saying, "At the foot of the statue of Lafayette, who fought in this country for liberty, I ask for liberty today."

One of the banners quoted President Wilson's war message, reading, "We shall fight for the things we hold nearest to our hearts—for democracy, for the right of those who submit to authority to have a voice in their own governments." The police considered the banners seditious and arrested the women for holding a public assembly on government property without a permit.

A *Washington Post* reporter covering Hunkins' arrest along with the other women in Lafayette Square asked Hunkins "why she and other suffragists were making laughingstocks of themselves." Hunkins responded that women had for years been patiently standing at the doors of Congress and petitioning for legislative relief. Now women were demanding action.

Helena Hill Weed was one of the suffragists jailed under harsh conditions. PHOTOGRAPH COURTESY OF THE LIBRARY OF CONGRESS, MNWP-275-275034U.

"Reforms of every other kind have been set aside and buried under the plea of war necessities," Hunkins said, "but instead of allowing suffrage to be smothered we are taking advantage of the war situation to point out that if this war is for democracy, if we are to send our soldiers 3,000 miles into the trenches of a foreign land to fight for democracy, it would not be amiss to have democracy extended at home."

Hunkins was unbowed and seemingly indefatigable. In an August 15, 1918, telegram to Mrs. E. L. Perkins in Billings, Hunkins wrote cheerily, "Twenty-six of America's finest women are accompanying me to jail. It's splendid. Don't worry. Love Hazel."

The banners and the protests and the arrests proved effective, eventually. Following the end of the war, on June 4, 1919, Congress approved the Susan B. Anthony Amendment providing for women's suffrage. On August 18, 1920, the 19th Amendment, providing full voting rights for women nationally, was ratified. This culminated a forty-two-year effort in Congress from when the amendment was first introduced, but the push for equality dates back to before the nation's founding, as documented in the writings of Abigail Adams and Phyllis Wheatley.

The 19th Amendment was a major achievement, but not all women benefited. Jim Crow laws still prevented many Black women from voting, and Native Americans—men and women—were not recognized as citizens until passage of the Snyder Act in 1924. In many states, they remained disenfranchised until the Voting Rights Act of 1965 was passed.

Within a little over three months of this momentous electoral victory, Hunkins was off to her next challenge. In a 1920 news article, "Where Are the Suffragettes," by George B. Waters, she was one of six prominent suffragists who were moving on to other work. "Hazel Hunkins, Billings, Mont., has sailed for England to make a study of the cooperative movement and will soon return with her information to be given to groups of farmers and workers."

A 1922 article in the *Burlington Free Press and Times* listed her among ten militant suffragists who married shortly after the suffrage amendment passed. The *Free Press and Times* incorrectly wrote that she had married an English man, Timothy Hallinan.

The article named her as one of six suffragists in Alice Paul's "army" who could be "depended on for a real demonstration and hunger strike in prison . . . all of whom served terms in jail and refused to eat. The principal bit of jewelry worn by each of the young women is the little jail door pin."

In reality, Hunkins didn't wed until 1930, when she married journalist Charles Thomas "Timothy" Hallinan. Born in Michigan, he worked as a journalist in England and was a prominent pacifist. They had four children together, with three of them born before their marriage, according to her personal papers.

Hunkins-Hallinan worked as a freelance journalist in England, writing a column under the pseudonym Ann Whittingham (a variation on her mother's maiden name) for the *Chicago Tribune*, focusing on English society and Americans in England. She also became very active in the British feminist organization, the Six Point Group, where she served in numerous leadership offices, including chair. The group's name stemmed from the six legislative issues it worked on: (1) to address child assault, (2) to help widowed mothers, (3) to help unmarried single mothers and their children, (4) to attain equal guardianship rights for men and women, (5) to secure equal pay for teachers, and (6) to secure equal pay and opportunities for men and women in the civil service. These six points evolved to be six general points of equality for women: political, occupational, moral, social, economic, and legal.

In an introduction to a Six Point Group book, *In Her Own Right*, that she edited, Hunkins-Hallinan wrote, "We claim for every woman the chance to develop as a person *in her own right*."

She never abandoned working for women's equality. In a 1980 interview, a *Los Angeles Times* reporter described her as "baffled" as to why the Equal Rights Amendment was not ratified. "I'm afraid there are just too many people who thought it was the end of the fight when the voting rights amendment was approved," Hunkins-Hallinan said. "But there is still deep-seated discrimination. We have to have the ERA." In 1977, she returned to the

United States to participate in a march for the Equal Rights Amendment. She was a guest of honor at the White House, and President Carter signed a Women's Equality Day Proclamation and gave her the pen.

On May 17, 1982, Hazel Hunkins-Hallinan died from respiratory failure at her home in North London at the age of ninety-one. She was buried at Mountainview Cemetery in Billings next to her husband, who died in 1971, and her parents.

CHAPTER 6

Modern Warrior Fought to Protect the Crow Tribe: Robert Yellowtail

"*We love our country because it is beautiful, because we are born here. Strangers will . . . try to possess it as surely as the sun will come tomorrow.*"

Such were the prescient and ominous words of the great Crow chief Plenty Coups. In many ways, they define the ongoing battle lines faced by the Crow down through the centuries and to this day.

One of the Crow leaders who stepped up to stop the U.S. government, settlers, and corporations from stealing and plundering their land was Robert Summers Yellowtail, Sr., who would become a longtime tribal leader of the Crow during the twentieth century.

"Autonomy . . . Autonomy . . . Autonomy."

These were the words Yellowtail delivered in a cadence matching the pounding of his twisted walking stick as he addressed the Crow tribal council. With solemnity, he reminded tribal members of their struggle for sovereignty and their decades-long fight over the damming of the Bighorn River. (Historian Megan Benson, whose work has focused on tribal rights and water resources, ably described the tribe's struggles in a two-part article, "The Fight for Crow Water," in the Winter 2007 and Spring 2008 issues of *Montana, The Magazine of Western History*.) The dam would prevail, built forty-four miles south of Hardin, Montana. Ironically, it would bear his name, although Yellowtail fiercely opposed its construction for decades.

The fight for Crow autonomy and sovereignty was a theme that ran through Yellowtail's life. He would take his place in the front lines of his first battle to defend Crow lands when he was in his twenties, standing in the halls of Congress.

The Crow's rich lands in south-central Montana along the Bighorn River have long drawn the covetous eyes of Whites, dating back to the times of early fur traders in 1805. The tribe calls themselves *Apsáalooke*, which means "children of the large-beaked bird."

Robert Yellowtail's leadership protected Crow lands and autonomy.
PHOTOGRAPH BY KENNETH F. ROAHEN, COURTESY OF THE BUD LAKE AND RANDY BREWER CROW INDIAN PHOTOGRAPH COLLECTION, MONTANA HISTORICAL SOCIETY RESEARCH CENTER ARCHIVES.

Early White people translated it as "Crow." One of the first visitors to write about the tribe was Francis La Rocque of the Northwest Fur Company, based in Montreal. La Rocque lived with them for two months and found them to be shrewd traders, expert horsemen, and clever hunters. La Rocque also saw that their hunting grounds had abundant game. (These details from La Rocque's writing were uncovered by William M. Brooke and featured in his senior honors thesis at Carroll College in Helena.)

In 1806, during the Corps of Discovery's homeward return on the Yellowstone River, William Clark remarked on the land's riches in his journal and noted the navigable waters and plentiful timber. He thought it an ideal place for a trading post.

During the next two decades, more expeditions crossed Crow lands, likewise noting the area's abundant wildlife. As years passed, more Whites surged West, particularly with the settling of the Oregon Territory in the 1830s and the California gold rush of 1849.

When tensions mounted on the Plains between Whites and tribes, the U.S. government negotiated a treaty in 1851 at Fort Laramie with several Plains tribes and promised to compensate them for the migrations through their lands.

These incursions, however, marked but the opening volleys in an unrelenting onslaught as Whites poured into Crow territory and continually pressured government officials to reduce tribal lands and resources. Through a series of treaties and other agreements, beginning in 1851 and continuing to 1904, Crow territory was slashed from 38 million acres to less than 3 million, with little of value given to the Crow in return.

The decade Yellowtail was born, the 1880s, coincided with the tribe's relocation and confinement within the boundaries of a reservation that was but a small remnant of the vast, abundant landscape that was once "Crow Country." Although their territory was rapidly shrinking, the Crow continued their lifestyle of hunting buffalo and living off the land. And surprisingly, throughout much of their history, they maintained non-hostile, even friendly, relations with Whites.

In 1875, Crow chief Plenty Coups saw what was happening in the Black Hills gold rush and spoke of "the yellow metal that drives the white man mad." He predicted the Whites would overrun "the sacred mountains of the Sioux and that will bring war." He decided the Crow should align with the Whites and be their scouts in order to better protect Crow lands. "And when the war is over, the soldier-chiefs will not forget that the Crows came to their aid. I—Plenty Coups—will not let them forget." (As this chapter later explains, they would indeed forget decades later—particularly when coveting Crow resources for a dam project during the administration of that famous soldier-chief Dwight Eisenhower, who was U.S. president from 1953 to 1961.)

A decade after Plenty Coups' observation, alarming events were unfolding in Washington, D.C. In 1887, President Grover Cleveland signed the General Allotment Act (also known as the Dawes Severalty Act of 1887), which aimed to turn the Crow and other tribes into farmers.

According to the *Encyclopedia of Minorities in American Politics,* under the Dawes Act, between 1887 and 1934, Native Americans "lost control of about 100 million acres of land" or about "two-thirds of the land base they held in 1887." The result was devastating to tribes, including the Crow, stripping them not only of land, but also of their communal way of life and their very identities. Instead of land shared by the tribe for the well-being of all, their homelands were broken into parcels ranging from 40- to 320-acre allotments, with the remainder of the tribal land to be declared surplus and sold to non-natives, railroads, and large corporations.

Senator Henry Dawes, the author of the act, argued that it was time to "rid the nation of tribalism through the virtues of private property, allotting land parcels to Indian heads of family." While he and others apparently saw the law as a way to "assimilate" American Indians into White culture, others saw it for what it truly was—a land grab.

One of the more vocal opponents of Dawes' plan, Senator Henry M. Teller of Colorado, said it was a way "to despoil the Native Americans of their lands and to make them vagabonds on the face of the earth." Congressman Russell Errett said that:

> **the real aim was to get at the Indian lands and open them up to settlement. The provisions for the apparent benefit of the Native Americans are but the pretext to get at his lands and occupy them. . . . If this were done in the name of Greed, it would be bad enough; but to do it in the name of Humanity . . . is infinitely worse.**

—ʬ—

Few U.S. policies were as destructive to Native American society as the Dawes Act. It was signed into law about the same time Robert Yellowtail was born on the Crow Reservation. (He was likely born in 1889, but church records indicate 1887.)

As a child, Yellowtail saw the Crow's very way of life and survival "extinguished," undermining their value system, according to journalist and filmmaker Connie Poten. They lost their self-sufficiency, their lifestyle, and their freedom of movement. They even lost their identities. Agency regulations required them to use English names that would be passed on to future generations, rather than names in their own language more fitting to their lives and character.

Yellowtail was just four years old when he was taken from his parents by White Arm, a member of the Indian office of local police, and "incarcerated" in a Crow Reservation boarding school. There he was prevented from practicing his religion and speaking his own language.

Although he was upset with how the boarding school treated students, he never resisted schooling. "He was fascinated by the world of learning," Poten wrote. "Yellowtail pleaded to be sent to a better school, and Indian Agent Major Samuel Reynolds enrolled him in the Sherman Institute in Riverside, California," where Yellowtail studied for eight years.

In 1907, he graduated from the high school division and began studying law with a local justice of the peace. "His dream was to become a lawyer," wrote his biographer Tim Bernardis. Returning to Montana around 1910, he hoped to attend law school but life intervened. Historians and news reports disagree on whether Yellowtail actually earned a law degree. One account reported he finally earned it through correspondence classes from the University of Chicago, but Bernardis believes this is more legend than fact.

"It was a deep feeling stirring around inside of me," Yellowtail recalled at age ninety-three. "I studied the law because I was disgusted with the way Indian Affairs was being administered in Washington. I said to myself,

'I'm going to make this my life's work, graduate in law, and defend the Indians,'" Poten recounted.

When the battle lines were drawn in 1917, young Yellowtail went up against one of Congress' most skilled attorney members, Senator Thomas Walsh of Montana. In 1910, Walsh had introduced a bill to open Crow lands to homesteaders, arguing that the Crow Tribe didn't need the land. He claimed that the dwindling Crow Tribe proved that the "communistic tribal system ought, in the interests of the Indians, to be abandoned as speedily as possible." (The Crow population had declined from 3,500 in 1887 to 1,710, but by 2022, there were 14,280 enrolled members of the tribe, with about 7,900 living on the reservation that Yellowtail fought so hard to preserve.)

While Yellowtail was in California, parts of the reservation had been "allotted" under a Crow compromise to the Dawes Act and assigned to individual tribal members. The government and folks like Senator Walsh and the Montana delegation now saw an opportunity to declare some of the land "surplus" and sell it to White settlers, according to Bernardis and Frederick Hoxie.

The land war between Congress and the Crow lasted at least nine years, says Bernardis, from 1908 to 1917. On April 5, 1917, the night before the final hearing in Congress, Chief Plenty Coups and four other Crow chiefs called a War Medicine session in their room at the National Hotel in Washington, D.C., Yellowtail wrote in an account years later. Burning sweetgrass and buffalo chips (which they acquired from the National Zoological Park), the chiefs recounted the many Crow victories and defeats of their long war history against various tribes. Plenty Coups said that all the previous battles had been on equal terms, but now they were going up against an enemy "far superior in numbers, on his own ground and terms . . . not with guns, but by argument of mouth, and in a language and on terms which we did not understand," wrote Yellowtail. The Crow chiefs prayed to the Great Spirit for help, with all of them blessing Yellowtail. That night, Chief Plenty Coups chose Yellowtail to speak for the tribe and save its land because the chiefs could not speak or understand the language used in Congress.

According to Yellowtail, when choosing him to represent the tribe, Plenty Coups said, "This is a contest of words with whitemen, in a whitemen's court with whitemen sitting in judgment of us." Biographers Frederick Hoxie and Tim Bernardis wrote that Yellowtail's "oratorical powers in both the Crow and English language were renowned, recalling the skill of orator chiefs in the buffalo days." They described him as "high-strung and impatient, flamboyant and bombastic," with "an excellent command of the English language, both oral and written" and "extensive knowledge of the law."

The day Woodrow Wilson declared war on the Central Powers, April 6, 1917, Yellowtail, Plenty Coups, and the Crows finally prevailed. It was an incredible moment in Crow history and in Yellowtail's career. He was told he had only eighteen minutes to make his case, but he took four and a half hours. During his final argument, Yellowtail cited the Constitution, the Crow's history of giving sanctuary to Whites, and the Northwest Ordinance of 1787, which promised, "The utmost good faith shall always be observed toward Indians; their lands and property shall never be invaded or taken from them without their consent."

He also levied a blistering attack against government officials—specifically the Secretary of the Interior and the Commissioner of Indian Affairs—for leaving the Crow to fight for their lives in this hearing without the assistance of an attorney. Yellowtail later compared this David and Goliath mismatch to that of an amateur boxer going up against the world champion.

At the closure of the hearing, following a break for committee members to vote on declaring war against Germany, five of the committee members pledged a two-week filibuster against passage of Walsh's bill. Walsh withdrew it.

Yellowtail was twenty-eight at the time of his victory. It must have been quite the fascinating scene. Watching the hearing with avid interest were not only 19 members of the Crow delegation, but as many as 200 members of other tribes, including two Osage chiefs in their native garb, all anxious to see what fate would befall the Crow.

As Bernardis and Hoxie wrote, "In later years, [Crow war chief, author, and historian] Joseph Medicine Crow summed up the significance of Yellowtail's actions, saying that Yellowtail 'saved our reservation . . . he has been a warrior. . . . That's why we are still Crow Indians to this day.'" Yellowtail himself wrote of that day's significance, saying, "It is impossible for [young Crow and future generations] to appreciate how close to complete obliteration by political connivement they came to that day."

At the close of the hearing, Chief Plenty Coups reportedly stood up and pointed his cane at Senator Walsh, as if counting coup.

In addition to his great oratorical skills, Bernardis and Hoxie wrote that "Yellowtail also possessed certain personal characteristics that served him well; he was remarkably intelligent, shrewd, dynamic, and humorous. He could also be very precise and businesslike." These abilities and gifts earned him both admiration by some and the enmity of jealous tribal members, suspicious of his ability to move deftly in the White world as well as on the reservation, according to Poten. Bernardis found that these contrasting opinions of him still remain today, decades after his death.

His critics saw him as "ill-tempered, a bully, and working primarily for his own interests," wrote Charles Crane Bradley, Jr., a tribal historian, "but his lifelong consistently stated goals were for human rights, self-determination, tribal autonomy, and economic rehabilitation for his people. While people suspected Yellowtail of working for his own interest, his political activities more than amply rewarded the Crow tribe."

Two years after his victory, Yellowtail was back in Washington, D.C., this time advocating to Congress for the new Crow Allotment Act, which he had helped draft, and much, much more. He gave an impassioned speech to the Senate Committee on Indian Affairs on September 9, 1919, demanding autonomy for American Indians. He said that

> **the American Indian, also a creature of God, claims, as you yourselves do, to be endowed with certain inalienable rights, among which are life, liberty, and the pursuit of happiness. He further maintains as his inherent right to choose the manner in which he shall seek his own happiness. . . .**
>
> **I hold that the Crow Indian Reservation is a separate semi-sovereign nation in itself, not belonging to any State, nor confined with the boundary lines of any State of the Union, and that until such proper cessions, as had been agreed to and as expressed in our covenant, have been duly complied with no Senator, or anybody else, so far as that is concerned, has any right to claim the right to tear us asunder by the continued introduction of bills here without our consent. . . .**

He chastised the committee for treating "sacred covenants" as mere "scraps of paper," adding that the United States had been holding itself up as a champion of democracy during the recent World War, but that apparently these concerns for the health of democracy were never meant to apply to the North American Indian.

He reminded the committee members it was the Crow who served as scouts for the U.S. military, "and in doing so risked their lives to assist you, when you were sorely in need." He also told the committee that nothing in the treaties or "sacred covenants" referred to any agreements whereby the state could "take or sell any portions of our lands" or to set aside lands "against our wishes" for other purposes.

It would be 1924 before the Snyder Act guaranteed American Indians full citizenship, but they would not be eligible to vote in every state until 1965, when the Voting Rights Act passed.

Fifteen years after Yellowtail's fiery demand for tribal autonomy, the Commissioner of Indian Affairs selected Yellowtail as the Crow Reservation's superintendent. Yellowtail was the first Native American to earn such an honor. As one of Yellowtail's biographers, Frederick Hoxie, noted, "It marked the start of a new era in which the tribe would be able to speak for itself and chart its own course in American history."

The 1920 Crow Allotment Act was but a stopgap measure to protect Crow lands. Unfortunately, the tribe may have missed an opportunity for better protection of tribal land with the Indian Reorganization Act under the Roosevelt administration, but they voted it down on May 18, 1935, because of their distrust of the federal government, according to Charles Crane Bradley, Jr., who wrote an unpublished history of the tribe in 1974 for the Tribal Culture Committee. The reorganization plan just came at the wrong time because of the hard-fought battles the Crow had just endured with Washington.

The tribe lost out on better protection of tribal land, as well as important federal funding for education and agricultural and industrial projects. The worst thing about the Crow Act, Bernardis said, were amendments that opened the door for leasing land to non-Indians.

THE DAM FIGHT

A new major battle was brewing—once again Whites and the U.S. government lusted for Crow lands. The government pushed to build a monumental dam on the Bighorn River, a river held sacred by the Crow. According to Poten, the Bighorn was considered "the Crow's lifeblood and where Chief Plenty Coups had killed his first Sioux."

The push for the dam dated back decades, beginning in 1905 when the U.S. Reclamation Service (forerunner to the Bureau of Reclamation) first proposed the project. In 1935, Montana Governor Frank Cooney promoted the idea. By the end of World War II, the federal government was looking at the Bighorn River as a source of hydropower and irrigation water.

Bighorn Canyon is sacred Crow land. PHOTOGRAPH BY ZACK FRANK, COURTESY OF SHUTTERSTOCK.

Yellowtail, who had resigned from his Bureau of Indian Affairs (BIA) position in 1945 and was tribal chairman at this time, led the tribal council to vote 80 to 1 against the dam. But the U.S. Bureau of Reclamation ignored this vote and pressed for negotiations on 7,000 acres of Crow land, but Yellowtail refused. The federal government valued the land at a mere $1.5 million, while the Crow set the value at $5 million. As Plenty Coups had warned, many people coveted Crow land. This time it was energy companies, as well as Whites in nearby communities.

They wanted a dam for flood control, electricity, recreation, and irrigation. To get what they wanted, Connie Poten wrote, they "ignored Congressional promises to hold treaty lands in trust for Indians' best interests."

Yellowtail was forced to negotiate and asked the government to lease the land for $1 million per year for fifty years, and to then turn over the dam to the Crow Tribe. The Crow Tribe unanimously approved a resolution to this effect, but in response, Montana Senator James Murray threatened to condemn the river to take federal control.

The Crow feared they would lose their tribal status and thus their land. In 1953, the U.S. House passed House Concurrent Resolution 108, which called for the termination of tribal status for selected tribes and removing their lands from protection. President Eisenhower himself apparently endorsed this approach. Between 1953 and 1964, more than 100 tribes and bands lost federal recognition as sovereign nations. More than 12,000 Native Americans lost their tribal status, and 2.5 million acres of tribal lands were removed from protection, much of it sold to non-Indians.

Another ominous turn was government duplicity. As Poten reported, government men spread rumors that Yellowtail had made a secret deal about the dam. A Bureau of Reclamation official threw gas on the fire by naming the dam after Yellowtail, further stirring up suspicions and jealousies among tribal members. Another Reclamation official told a White rancher to offer Yellowtail a $21,000 bribe to give up his fight against the dam.

But Yellowtail turned the tables on them by reporting it to the FBI. He then went on a radio program in Billings, decrying the ploy and calling it "a day of infamy." Government officials also knocked on doors of tribal members, promising them money if they would vote to sell the area needed for the dam.

The tribal council finally voted to sell the dam site for $5 million, and Congress approved the deal in 1956. Yellowtail appealed to President Eisenhower to veto the deal, but his efforts backfired. Eisenhower did veto the deal, on the grounds that it was an "extravagant" cost. Instead, he signed an agreement to pay the tribe only half of the agreed-upon amount, a total of $2.5 million. Yellowtail had "lost the battle." His arguments were dismissed by Congress and the courts, recounted Poten. He also lost the support of the Crow people, who voted to sell the land. One of his own sons voted to sell the dam site because his mother advised him to take thc $600 a government man had promised him for college.

Following appeals, the government got the land, approval to build the dam, and all future proceeds from the dam for only $2.5 million. Each tribal member received $600. A last-minute amendment allowed the tribe to sue for the balance of the original $5 million. In 1962, a judge awarded the tribe an additional $2 million, but half of that went to attorney's fees, according to Poten.

The dam opened in 1964, becoming the largest electricity producer in the Missouri River basin. This defeat must have been particularly painful for Yellowtail and his supporters. A headline in the *Hardin Herald* boasted, "Crow Scalps Hang on Yellowtail Dam."

Yellowtail said, "It's the same old story. To hell with the Indians, take their land and talk afterwards." Not only had the Crow lost the battle, but thanks to government interference the tribe was bitterly divided for years to come, so much so that their beloved Crow Fair, which Yellowtail himself fostered into a vital community event, was split into two events for years. The divide has never healed, says Bernardis, with reverberations that last to the present day.

Despite the dam defeat, Yellowtail continued to fight for his people. In the 1970s, during the Arab oil embargo, the nation's attention again turned to Crow land, this time eyeing its coal reserves. The tribe owned one-fifth of the strippable coal in the West, an estimated 17 billion tons.

Yellowtail united the tribe to reject an offer from the BIA in favor of a better contract with Westmoreland Coal Company. It was also Yellowtail who inquired about who would be collecting the tax revenues from the subsurface coal in land that had been ceded to the federal government, according to Poten and Bernardis. Montana had already collected $30 million in revenue before the Crow entered the legal battle to protect their mineral rights.

In January 1988, the U.S. Supreme Court concurred with a lower court ruling, siding with the Crow. The tribe would receive the $30 million from the state, plus $4 million annually.

Over the decades, Yellowtail had done a great deal to help his tribe thrive. During his time as tribal superintendent, he stocked the reservation with buffalo from Yellowstone National Park, used federal funds to build up high-quality horse and cattle breeding stock on the reservation, and built a Crow hospital. In encouraging Crow culture and pride, he'd "resurrected" the Crow Fair, the Crow's popular summer powwow. In an essay in the *Tribal College Journal of American Indian Higher Education*, Steven Crum credits Yellowtail for championing Native American higher education through securing scholarships, advocating for higher education, and seeking federal education grant funds. Crum also notes that Yellowtail was an early advocate for the Crow Tribe establishing Little Big Horn College, which was chartered by the tribe in 1980.

Although Yellowtail accomplished much, he was not without his critics over the decades. Multiple complaints had been submitted about him to the Office of the Commissioner of Indian Affairs, mostly concerning his endorsement of ceremonial peyote and his "haphazard approach to tribal accounting." The General Accounting Office annually asked him for clarifications regarding irregularities such as cash transfers from one Indian's account to another, missing vouchers, and failure to itemize individual Indian accounts. As recounted by historian Megan Benson, Yellowtail's successor claimed it took years to reconcile the agency books. None of the complaints led to formal charges, but the controversies did poison some relationships and detract from his legacy.

Biographer Bernardis said, "I think he's both well thought of and not so well thought of here today on the reservation." Some people thought he got favors from big lessees. "But my way of thinking," said Bernardis, "what he did fighting the opening of the reservation was maybe his most important legacy. I think the man did a great thing by fighting [it]. What he did was good. He stopped the general opening [of the reservation to land grabs]." Over the years, however, Bernardis said, non-tribal lessees have found ways to take advantage of tribal landowners who needed money.

Bernardis and Hoxie noted that despite defeats, Yellowtail "consistently used both his Crow cultural ties and the skills he learned in boarding school to establish a different type of leadership in the new era of reservation life."

Robert Yellowtail relaxes with his family in 1941. PHOTOGRAPH COURTESY OF THE UNIVERSITY OF TEXAS AT ARLINGTON LIBRARY SPECIAL COLLECTIONS.

His skills were not of the battlefield, but of those honed for verbal and political battles in tribal council chambers, courtrooms, and Congress.

"In his struggle he helped the Crows endure the white invasion and become 'a separate, semi-sovereign nation' within the United States," wrote Bernardis and Hoxie in *The New Warriors*.

Robert Summers Yellowtail, Sr., ninety-eight, died on June 18, 1988, at his home in Lodge Grass. Though not all his efforts proved successful, Robert Yellowtail did live up to his personal focus and goal: "When I go to meet Plenty Coups in the sky," he said, "I want to be able to tell him that our Crow people are in good shape."

— CHAPTER 7 —

Nursing Trailblazer: Susie Walking Bear Yellowtail

Born near Pryor, Montana, on the Crow Indian Reservation, Susie Walking Bear grew up in a sod-roofed cabin with a dirt floor.

This shy young girl from humble roots would grow up to be a registered nurse and a powerful woman who confronted Indian Health Service (IHS) abuses and would speak out for humane treatment of the Crow and other American Indians. She blew the whistle on the IHS's involuntary sterilizations of American Indian women. She spoke up demanding that Native people be treated as human beings with respect and dignity. She became fearless, but she also paid a price.

Susie Walking Bear Yellowtail "was very much a trailblazer in the field of Native nursing," wrote author Brianna Theobald in her book, *Reproduction on the Reservation: Pregnancy, Childbirth, and Colonialism in the Long Twentieth Century*.

Tribal historian Joe Medicine Crow said at the time of Yellowtail's death in 1981, "The Indian peoples, particularly the Crow Tribe, lost a dedicated and forceful spokeswoman. Her voice rang out strong and clear at meetings, conferences, and seminars throughout the country. When she talked, people—both Indian and non-Indian—listened. Why? Because this woman spoke with experience, knowledge, and conviction about the poor health conditions of the Indians and how to make them healthy and strong once again. She also had great concern for the education of her Indian people."

Many photos of Susie show her with laughing, smiling eyes. She was known for her easygoing manner, irreverent and captivating wit, and her husky laugh.

Susie Walking Bear was born on January 27, 1903. Her mother, Jane White Horse (also known as Kills the Enemy), was Oglala Sioux. Her father, Walking Bear, was *Apsáalooke* (Crow). He died before she was born, and she was raised by her mother and stepfather Stone Breast. At age eight, she began attending the Catholic Mission in Pryor and later switched to the government boarding school at Crow Agency.

When she was twelve, she was orphaned when her mother died, and Susie was sent to the Indian boarding school in Lodge Grass, Montana. The death of her mother would influence Susie's advocacy for youth later in life.

"I was the biggest tomboy" at the boarding school, she recalled in an interview with Ann Gorzalka that was published in *Country Journal* after Susie's death. "But I sometimes wondered how we got through. We weren't allowed to speak our own tongue or even think in it . . . they washed out our mouths with homemade grease and lye soap whenever they caught us talking Indian."

"I remember one time in particular, when I was severely punished for speaking Crow. They made me kneel for several hours on a broomstick in a corner of the laundry. I passed out several times. Each time they picked me up and put me on the broomstick. It was terrible, but that's what actually happened," she told Gorzalka.

She also recounted working in the kitchen at one of the boarding schools where she saw a lot of delicious food—but the chicken and jelly and butter and cream were all for staff and none went to the children. "We had oatmeal with skim milk." And once a day they ate terrible tasting boiled meat.

That school taught only to sixth grade. In 1919, at age sixteen, Susie left home to attend a boarding school off the reservation. There, according to historian Brianna Theobald, Susie and other Crow students were recruited by missionary Francis Shaw to accompany her to a Baptist convention in Denver. Apparently

Shaw had told Susie she could return to the Crow Reservation, but then Shaw instead "persuaded" Susie to accompany her to Muskogee, Oklahoma, to attend Bacone Indian School, where she completed her eighth-grade studies.

Francis Shaw married Clifford Field, and in the early 1920s she brought Susie to the Northfield Seminary in Massachusetts. Field paid the girl's tuition, but Susie worked as a nanny and maid to earn room and board. Balancing school work with the load of housework and childcare was grueling, according to Kathryn A. Askins in her history dissertation, "Bridging Cultures: American Indian Students at the Northfield Mount Hermon School."

Askins wrote that Susie walked a mile to school in the morning, then returned a mile to prepare and care for the Field children's lunch, then walked back to school, and then home again to prepare the children's evening meal, in addition to carrying a full course load.

The school administrators treated her poorly, and refused to let Susie use her full last name, Walking Bear, insisting she drop her last name or change it. Susie shortened it to Bear.

Her employers also treated her with suspicion. Her relationship with Shaw soured. Susie later recounted that Shaw "lost her missionary spirit somewhere along the way" and told Susie, "You're nothing but an Indian."

Susie ran away and joined a friend in New York or Philadelphia (accounts vary). The friend convinced her to return, telling her, "Susie, you have to stick it out. You have to show them you are somebody." After Susie graduated, she decided to train as a nurse, which would give her independent income and an opportunity to help her people. Her boarding school education had primarily trained her to be a housemaid and nanny; undertaking a nursing education would be a major challenge. Her aunt, who lived on the Crow Reservation, had taken over guardianship of her when Susie's mother died, demanded she return to the reservation and get married. Susie refused.

Other Baptist sponsors stepped up, and Susie enrolled in the Franklin County Public Hospital nursing program in Greenfield, Massachusetts,

Susie Walking Bear, rear row, center, poses with other graduates of the 1927 class of Boston City Hospital's School of Nursing. PHOTOGRAPH COURTESY OF THE MONTANA HISTORICAL SOCIETY RESEARCH CENTER ARCHIVES.

where she trained with Dr. Halbert Stetson. She continued her education at Boston City Hospital's School of Nursing, "one of the oldest and most prestigious nursing schools in the country," writes Theobald, and graduated with honors in 1927, becoming the first Crow registered nurse. She was among a mere handful of American Indians who became trained nurses during this era.

Susie returned briefly to work at Franklin Hospital in Greenfield, and then, a year after graduating from nursing school, she joined the Indian Health Service (IHS) and returned to the Crow Reservation. She worked for a short time as a supervisory nurse at the Crow Agency Hospital, where she had a "brief and overwhelmingly negative employment" experience, according to Theobald.

Theobald writes that Susie's decision to resign "was prompted by her complete and total frustration with the hospital's White employees." As a registered nurse at the Crow Agency Hospital, she "would have it out with the doctors. . . . It was just really bad," Susie recounted in an interview decades later. "I'd tell those doctors 'Just because we're Indians doesn't mean you can do this to us. You think you can get away with it, but finally someone is here who knows what is going on.'"

One frustrating incident she shared dealt with a senior physician, Ira Nelson, who had worked on the reservation for more than a decade. A Crow woman was at the hospital, in labor, but Nelson refused to come to the hospital to deliver the baby. Susie delivered the baby herself, but Nelson rushed in at the last minute and cut the umbilical cord too short, causing complications. Susie had to take extraordinary steps to save the baby's life.

Adding to her frustration, the White staff didn't speak the Native language or understand the culture of their Crow patients. Other battles with IHS centered on the involuntary sterilizations of Native women. Susie herself would eventually become one of the casualties.

Theobald also notes that Susie and other Native nurses did not rigidly separate indigenous healing practices from Western medicine and were known "to look the other way" when patients brought indigenous healing practices, including peyote, into the hospital.

Susie's time as "an insider" convinced her that Crows were commonly mistreated at the Crow Agency Hospital. Later conversations in her life indicate she observed doctors performing unethical sterilizations, but Theobald says the whereabouts of the medical records from her time working there in 1929 are unknown.

Those who knew Susie said that her stint at Crow Agency Hospital transformed her into a "lifelong activist," but her family tended to think of her as an advocate rather than an activist.

Susie left the Crow Agency Hospital in 1929, which was also the year she married Thomas Yellowtail. He would become a tribal spiritual leader and a leader of the Sun Dance. Thomas was also the brother of Robert Yellowtail, Sr., who was superintendent of the Crow Indian Reservation from 1934 to

1945 (see Chapter 6). Thomas revitalized many important Crow cultural practices such as the Sun Dance.

Susie with her husband, Tom Yellowtail, worked tirelessly to nourish Crow culture. PHOTOGRAPH COURTESY OF THE MONTANA HISTORICAL SOCIETY RESEARCH CENTER ARCHIVES.

After she quit working at the hospital, the administrators there labeled Susie a troublemaker and, despite Superintendent Yellowtail's efforts, she was unable to get health-related employment on the reservation throughout the 1930s.

Theobald writes that Yellowtail's experiences at Crow Agency influenced her own decisions about giving birth. For the birth of her first child, Virjama, she went to the hospital in Sheridan, Wyoming, and all went smoothly. The birth of her second child, Bruce, was a "nightmare" and took place at Crow Agency. It's suspected that the only reason she decided to use the Crow Agency Hospital was that the doctor there likely refused to approve paying for a birth at an off-reservation hospital, and Yellowtail and her husband couldn't afford to pay for the hospitalization.

The Crow Agency Hospital building at that time was described "as a horrible wreck." The hospital was designed for twelve beds but was packed with as many as thirty beds. It was also sometimes used as a jail for women.

And maternity patients were in close proximity to those with tuberculosis and other communicable diseases.

Susie later said, "The doctor was in such a rush [that] he didn't do too well by me . . . and I almost died."

Susie wasn't alone in raising an alarm about Indian healthcare. The 1928 Meriam Report, which was commissioned by the Institute for Government Research (later the Brookings Institution), was damning. It studied health, education, social, and industrial activities on reservations in twenty-three states and particularly criticized the Indian Health Service.

"The hospitals, salutatorian, and sanatorium schools maintained by the [Indian Health] Service, despite a few exceptions, must generally be characterized as lacking in personnel, equipment, management, and design," the Meriam Report stated. It also noted extreme poverty and lack of food on the reservations and criticized Indian boarding schools for providing poor nutrition and an inferior education for Indian students. The report further argued that staff were underpaid and, "in the case of doctors, the standards set for entrance are too low."

For her third child, Susie decided on a home birth and wrote a letter requesting that a government physician or field nurse attend, which was a practice allowed at that time. However, senior physician Charles Nagel wrote a hostile letter in response, stating he wouldn't authorize payment for such care. According to Theobald, some people conjectured that although Nagel didn't know Susie personally, his hostility may have been due to her "troublemaker" reputation.

Following the home birth, she developed a painful cyst on her ovary that needed to be surgically removed. Due to the intense pain, she finally went to the Crow Agency Hospital. As Theobald reports, Susie later said, "They were supposed to remove the cyst, but that doctor in Crow ended up sterilizing me and I didn't know it until he was through. He said, 'Three is all you want and three is all you're going to get.' I was so upset."

She maintained that her situation was not unique. While her sterilization took place during a gynecological surgery, she alleged that sterilization of Crow women without their consent was "routine practice"; it was "common government procedure back in those days." According to Theobald, doctors routinely tied women's fallopian tubes after they gave birth without getting their permission. The women discovered months later that they had been sterilized. Theobald compared what happened to Crow women to the so-called "Mississippi appendectomies" done to Black women in the South in the 1950s.

Susie particularly singled out Dr. Charles Nagel, who had sterilized her. Theobald says that "government records . . . confirm a high sterilization rate during his tenure at Crow." During the 1930s, "eugenic" surgeries flourished and, writes Theobald, "the decade witnessed the height of eugenic sterilizations."

In the United States, those who believed in eugenics used government-funded programs to control those they considered "undesirable populations," which included immigrants, poor people, people of color, unmarried mothers, the disabled, and those with mental illness. A disproportionate number of those sterilized were African American, Hispanic, and Native American.

Sterilizations of Native women continued nationally during the 1930s on reservations but declined in the 1940s, possibly because Americans were horrified at the Nazis' use of eugenics. There was also a general decline in the number of Native health facilities in the 1940s and 1950s. The 1950s were also a time when tribes across the country were fighting congressional termination of their tribal status. From 1953 to 1964, 109 tribes were terminated; more than 12,000 American Indians lost their reservations and tribal status.

Theobald credits Susie Yellowtail and other Native women for playing a role in the decline of sterilizations, saying, "The tireless work of women like Yellowtail as agitators and watchdogs cannot be discounted as an additional factor in limiting sterilizations in government hospitals." A friend who interviewed Susie about her life said that opposing forced sterilizations was what spurred Yellowtail's lifelong activism. Yellowtail is credited with playing a role in the removal of two of the "worst doctors" at Crow Agency.

A resurgence of sterilizations occurred nationally in the 1970s. Activists, health workers, and government investigators raised the alarm, accusing the U.S. government of genocide. In a 2016 Independent Lens documentary, Lisa Ko reported that, beginning in 1970, between 25 and 50 percent of Native women of childbearing age were sterilized during a six-year period. Among those speaking out during this period was Susie Yellowtail, who said, "to sterilize our women was to kill us."

Although Susie Yellowtail left Crow Agency Hospital in the 1920s, she never gave up working to improve Crow healthcare. She worked as a midwife from the 1930s through the 1950s. During the 1930s, she also reimmersed herself in Crow culture and, with her husband, took a leadership role in the Sun Dance ceremony, which was just returning to the reservation after being banned by the federal government for decades.

As a consultant for the Public Health Service (PHS), a forerunner of the U.S. Department of Health and Human Services, from the 1930s to the 1960s, Susie traveled to other reservations and reported "appalling living conditions" and healthcare needs. A 2007 profile on Susie Yellowtail in *The Chronicle of Nursing* notes, "Her investigations revealed many . . . injustices. In particular, it became evident that many seriously ill Navajo children were literally dying on their mothers' backs as the women walked as many as 20 miles toward the nearest hospital, seeking care for their child." She also advocated for cultural competency of healthcare workers on reservations and the need to reform IHS.

Montana historian Laura Ferguson wrote, "Yellowtail documented instances of Indian children dying from lack of access to medical care, Indian women being sterilized without consent, and tribal elders unable to communicate their health concerns to doctors."

At the request of PHS, a Crow Health Committee formed in 1956, which advocated for Crow health and the health of women and children. Susie Yellowtail became its first chair. According to Theobald, the committee's first report "insisted on the need for Indians to band together to secure their health and welfare, and the committee regularly coordinated with health committees throughout the region." Susie also advocated for patients. In 1961, President John Kennedy appointed her to the Surgeon General's Committee on Indian Health, giving her a national platform. Both the Johnson and Nixon administrations continued her appointment. She traveled all over Indian Country, making recommendations about Indian health. She also spoke directly to the president about "atrocities" that had taken place on the Crow Reservation decades earlier.

Despite problems with the Crow Agency Hospital, the Crow Health Committee supported the hospital. They knew that the reservation could lose the hospital, as other reservations had. Susie investigated other reservations' health concerns and realized that conditions at the Crow Agency Hospital were common in Indian Country.

Yellowtail also founded the first professional association of Native American nurses and was instrumental in securing tribal and governmental funding to train Native nurses. She advocated for other Native Americans to enter into the healthcare profession so they would speak up for their people.

Beyond Susie Yellowtail's intense involvement in healthcare, she lived a multi-faceted and rich life immersed in Crow culture. As a Crow dancer, she and Thomas and other Crow dancers were invited as cultural ambassadors to perform on a State Department tour in cities all over Europe, the Middle East, and North Africa in the 1950s.

A 1969 article in *The Sheridan Press* reported she was traveling to England to appear in a play with only American Indian actors to help people better understand their culture.

She and Thomas were both deeply spiritual, and both were devout Baptists but also took part in Native American spiritual practices and ceremonies, such as the Sun Dance. In a 2011 story in the *Moscow-Pullman Daily News*, reporter Holly Bowen writes that they prayed to both Jesus and *Akbaatadia*, but kept those spiritual aspects of their lives separate. Ethnographer Rodney Frey, who worked with them in the 1970s, called it "an ambidextrous way of behaving."

During the 1950s, Susie Yellowtail, right, toured far from home as a cultural ambassador. PHOTOGRAPH COURTESY OF THE MONTANA HISTORICAL SOCIETY RESEARCH CENTER ARCHIVES.

Both Susie and Thomas were very involved in revitalization of Crow culture and ceremonies and, of course, were very active in Crow dancing. Susie was also known for her exquisite traditional Crow beadwork. Both were active in creating a cultural bridge with non-natives through their numerous outreach activities, including the annual All-American Indian Days in Sheridan, Wyoming.

Deeply committed to their family, they raised two daughters, one son, two adopted sons, and numerous tribally adopted sons, as well as dozens of grandchildren and great-grandchildren.

In 1962, President Kennedy awarded Susie the President's Award for Outstanding Nursing Care. And in 1970, she was one of five featured speakers in a "Health, Education, and Welfare" documentary concerning services provided to indigenous communities by IHS. She also served on the President's

Council on Indian Education and Nutrition; was a member of the U.S. Department of Health, Education and Welfare's Council on Indian Health; and a member of the President's Special Council on Aging.

Susie traveled all over the country and internationally, representing Native American culture and advocating for Native American healthcare and needs. In her role as spokeswoman for reservation Indians, she said, "The Indians' needs are many, but most urgent is the need for better education." In 1972, Montana Governor Forrest Anderson appointed her to serve on the State Advisory Council for Vocational Education.

Crow historian Joe Medicine Crow said there should be a special word for people like Susie Yellowtail, who easily moved back and forth between the White world and the Native American world.

In the final decades of her life, she worked to establish a Crow orphanage on the reservation so orphans wouldn't be forced to leave the tribe like she did as a child. However, this was one goal that eluded her before her death.

In 1978 the American Indian Nurses Association named her Grandmother of American Indian Nurses.

Susie Walking Bear Yellowtail died at her home in Wyola, Montana, on December 25, 1981. In 1987, she was named to Montana's "Gallery of Outstanding Montanans" in the State Capitol. In 2002, the American Nurses Association chose Susie Yellowtail as their first Native American inductee in its Hall of Fame.

It seems particularly fitting that the woman who was once ostracized as a troublemaker at the Crow Agency Hospital and blocked from working in the medical field on the reservation would rise to national fame, and that one day her photo would be displayed in the lobby of the hospital where she fought her first battles.

CHAPTER 8

"Onward and Upward": Nurse Octavia Bridgwater

"Onward and Upward," is the motto Octavia Bridgwater (spelled Bridgewater in some sources) coined while president of the Pleasant Hour Club, a group of Black women who met socially and politically in Helena, Montana. It's a fitting theme to the trajectory of her life and that of her family

Born on October 1, 1903, Octavia was the daughter of a former slave. She would become the first African-American nurse in Montana's Red Cross Nursing Service and was one of an elite handful of Black nurses initially chosen to serve in World War II as part of the Army Corps of Nurses. She would also play a leadership role, working for decades to fight racial discrimination in Montana and nationally.

The story of Octavia, her mother Mamie, and her father Samuel, and their extended family is a story of creating something from nothing—of finding the extraordinary in the seemingly ordinary. Of rising above racism and adversity and persisting even in the hardest and most discouraging of times.

Mamie was one of the founders of the Pleasant Hour Club (PHC), a Helena social group established in 1917, which became a member of the Montana Federation of Colored Women's Clubs. Octavia and Mamie and fellow members exerted steady pressure in Montana and nationally to end racial discrimination. Octavia's life and that of her parents provide a fascinating glimpse into the lives of early Black residents in Helena and Montana, as they made forever-forward steps to improve their lives and those of their descendants.

OCTAVIA'S EARLY LIFE

Octavia's father, Samuel, was born into slavery in Tennessee while the Civil War was raging. He would have been three years old when it ended.

As a teen, he enlisted in 1879 in the U.S. Army's Twenty-Fourth Infantry and had guessed his age to do so. Nine years later he wrote to the family of his former slave owner, inquiring about his birthday, and received a postcard telling him he was born on February 25, 1862.

That postcard would be all the written history Samuel had of his early life in Dixon Springs, Tennessee. As a child he was a house servant in the home of slave owner Amelia Bridgwater, census records show. He may have never known who his parents were, since they weren't listed on the census.

Samuel's postcard was passed down from generation to generation—as an improvised birth certificate—and it now resides at the Smithsonian's National Museum of American History with other family artifacts and papers in one of the largest archives produced by a Black family in the American West, according to historian Charnan Williams.

Born in Gallatin, Tennessee, in 1872, Octavia's mother, Mamie, was one of eight children. Her parents had been slaves, and her paternal grandmother had been born in Africa. After the Civil War and the rise of Jim Crow laws in the South, Mamie's parents, Levi and Emily "Emma" Anderson, homesteaded in Oklahoma in 1888 and owned a farm of 160 acres. A few years later, Mamie moved west to marry career Buffalo Soldier Samuel Bridgwater at Fort Huachuca, in Arizona Territory, in 1892. In 1902 she followed Samuel to Fort Harrison, Montana.

Historian Williams notes, "The entire family's westward migration, leaving behind the Jim Crow South, was compelled by their search for the promise of freedom." The family archive that Mamie and Octavia compiled over decades, which now resides at the Smithsonian, shows the family's economic advancement, but also the persistence of racism wherever they resided.

Samuel clearly valued his new freedoms and exercised them eagerly. Wherever he was stationed in the West, he voted. But while the West offered many freedoms, such as the absence of restrictions in Helena regarding where Blacks could live, there could still be flashes of racism. Some of this ambivalent racial history in Montana can be traced back decades to when Montana Territory became a magnet for thousands of secessionists during the Civil War era. They brought their racist attitudes with them and even passed a school segregation bill in 1872 (repealed in 1895). Blacks experienced some freedom in education and housing and in some job opportunities, yet faced social discrimination in restaurants, hotel accommodations, and professional opportunities.

During Samuel's career, the Bridgwaters were stationed at three western forts: Fort Huachuca in Arizona Territory, Fort Douglas in Utah, and Fort William H. Harrison in Helena, Montana. As Charnan Williams writes, "In what is a rare memoir from a buffalo soldier's wife, Mamie acknowledged that western military forts offered some relief from the racism to which she had been accustomed in the South."

"We never had a color line in these old army posts," wrote Mamie, "everybody was the same out here. If the fort had not been abandoned, I would have remained out among Uncle Sam's boys. I loved it," she wrote of Fort Harrison.

In many ways, the army was good to Samuel. He retired as a sergeant in 1906 after serving twenty-seven years and then became a cook at Fort Harrison. He had served stints in both Cuba and the Philippines, where he was injured during the Battle of San Juan Hill. He was frequently ill from wounds he'd received there, and Mamie cared for him. She also worked as a matron at the veterans' hospital at the fort and cared for their five children.

Samuel died on June 9, 1912, at age fifty, leaving Mamie to support and raise their five children, which she did by doing domestic work in Helena homes. At that time, there were 420 Black people living in Helena, representing 3.4 percent of the city's population.

A National Register of Historic Places (NRHP) write-up on Helena's Black heritage reports that "[t]he number of Blacks living in the Helena area at that time reflected the solidarity of the prosperous and comfortable African-American community. There were no segregated neighborhoods, Blacks lived throughout the community in a variety of neighborhoods." The NRHP essay continues:

> **Its active, civic-minded residents articulated and spoke through the voice of Joseph Bass' Montana-published newspaper [the] *Plaindealer*, protesting acts of prejudice and discrimination. One political organization, the Colored Progressive League, counted 60 active members who pledged to expel Black pimps, prostitutes, gamblers, and hustlers from their midst and to defend unjustly harassed local African Americans. Helena's vibrant Black community also enjoyed recitals, plays, socials, and formal debates staged by an active literary society.**

Mamie moved the family into a home at 502 Peosta Street in 1915, which she rented for ten years and then purchased for $800 in 1925. It remained their family home for sixty years. The house became a gathering place for the African-American community and the Broadwater neighborhood, as well as a hub for church activities. Mamie was clerk of the Ebenezer Baptist Church, which later became the Wilder Avenue Baptist Church. Through church, Mamie and Octavia were involved in a broader religious network of activism. Historian Williams notes that the church "mobilized Blacks in Helena and linked them to larger African-American organizations and movements across the nation."

OCTAVIA'S CAREER

The 1920 U.S. Census shows that, at age sixteen, Octavia followed her mother into domestic work, apparently dropping out of school. But she was back in school several years later. A 1923 Helena High School yearbook lists her as a sophomore, and she's in the photograph of the 1925 graduating class. This means she would have been twenty-two at the time of her graduation. Based on the photograph, historian Ellen Baumler says Octavia was the only Black student in her class and likely the oldest student as well. These dry facts alone help paint a portrait of her as a focused, determined, hardworking young woman who deeply valued furthering her education.

Unable to attend a nursing school in Montana, she enrolled in the Lincoln School for Nurses, a large training school for African-American nurses in New York City, graduating in August 1930. According to Williams, Lincoln was one of only a few nursing schools outside of the South that accepted Black students. She then attended the University of the State of New York, where she received her registered nurse's degree.

Undeterred by many obstacles, Octavia Bridgwater pioneered a path for black women to succeed as professional nurses. PHOTOGRAPH COURTESY OF JANET HARRELL-CAMPBELL.

After graduating, she returned to Helena and worked as a private duty nurse. The record is unclear how long this lasted. While one article noted she had worked in this capacity for a year, another October 4, 1942, Helena *Independent Record* article announced that Octavia was the first "Negro nurse" to enroll in the Red Cross Nursing Service in Montana and that she had been working as a private duty nurse for the past ten years. Ellen Baumler says it's quite likely Octavia was working in private duty jobs for a decade because Montana hospitals at that time wouldn't hire Black nurses.

In the 1942 *Independent Record* article, the Red Cross spokeswoman stated, "Colored nurses now serve with the colored Army units," adding that Bridgwater would be called to report within the next few months. But the U.S. military refused to assign Black nurses to care for White troops.

Nationally, Octavia was one of just 56 Black nurses selected from a pool of 9,000 Black nurses who applied to serve. She was assigned to Tuskegee Air Force Base, where Black U.S. Army Air Corps servicemen were stationed.

Octavia served as a U.S. Army nurse during World War II. PHOTOGRAPH COURTESY OF JANET HARRELL-CAMPBELL.

By the time she reported for duty, the quota of Black nurses had been raised to 160. At that time, Black nurses were assigned to segregated facilities serving Black troops or were assigned to care for captured German prisoners of war.

As casualties mounted near the end of the war, the U.S. military suffered a severe nursing shortage. President Roosevelt announced that he was about to draft 18,000 nurses unless volunteers stepped forward. The National Association of Colored Graduate Nurses, civil rights organizations, and Black Congressman Adam Clayton Powell denounced the decision, pointing out that 9,000 African American applicants for the Army Nurse Corps had been ignored. Powell stated:

> **It is absolutely unbelievable that in times like these, when the world is going forward, that there are leaders in our American life who are going backward. It is further unbelievable that these leaders have become so blindly and unreasonably un-American that they have forced our wounded men to face the tragedy of death rather than allow trained nurses to aid because these nurses' skins happen to be of a different color.**

—∾—

The bill to draft nurses was never passed. But it wasn't until later in the war that Black nurses were assigned to hospitals that cared for all military personnel, regardless of their race.

According to Baumler, Black nurses "realized if they were not allowed to serve in the military, [they] would never be integrated into the mainstream medical community." They mobilized, using Black media and also flooding Congress and the White House with letters and telegrams. "Octavia's voice was one of those that helped bring about the change," notes Baumler.

In 1948 President Truman signed Executive Order 9981 integrating the military. Black nurses serving the war effort faced racial discrimination. A nurse named Elinor Powell reported entering a Woolworths store in Phoenix,

Arizona, only to be refused service at the lunch counter. It is likely Octavia faced similar discrimination while stationed in Arizona and when she was assigned to Tuskegee Air Force Base in Alabama during the war.

By following in her father's footsteps and joining the military, however, Octavia found an opportunity to serve and aid fellow soldiers. It also helped her gain social recognition and economic standing in society. During World War II, female nurses were allowed the status of officers. Octavia earned the rank of first lieutenant and possibly captain (once again, the record isn't clear, but her grave marker gives her rank as first lieutenant). Her success helped pave the way for others to follow.

After the war, Octavia was hired by St. Peter's Hospital in Helena. From one account, it appears she was the only Black nurse there, working in the maternity department until she retired in the 1960s.

Her nursing care made a difference. "She'd get a ton of cards from all over," recalled her great-nephew, Dr. Jules Harrell, a psychology professor at Howard University. "People were very grateful for whatever she'd done." One of them was Barbara Creel.

As recounted in a 2015 *Independent Record* story, in August 1948, Creel gave birth to a daughter, Patty, at the old St. Peter's Hospital. After breastfeeding, the newborn developed severe diarrhea. Octavia was her nurse. Creel recalled Octavia telling the attending physician, Dr. Morris, "This baby is going to die unless you do something." Morris did an emergency blood transfusion and the baby began to recover. Patty survived and in 1970 married her high school sweetheart, Joe Mazurek, who served as Montana Attorney General from 1993 to 2000.

Bridgwater's great-niece, Janet Harrell-Campbell, a television producer in Washington, D.C., once received a blog posting from a woman who wrote, "One of the miracles in my life was Octavia Bridgwater."

The woman told of arriving at the hospital in 1947 in severe pain in labor with her first child. She was only seventeen years old. Her doctor arrived and blithely announced he was going out for a drive with his wife and would be back in a few hours.

Despite the young woman's pleadings, he headed out the door. Octavia "took me gently by the shoulders," the woman recalled, "and said 'Don't you worry. You're going to be okay. I'm going to get another doctor right now.'" Octavia stayed with her until the doctor she'd called had arrived. The young woman had already begun to give birth.

Longtime Helena resident and retired teacher Bonnie Bowler recalled that her mother, Edeen Bowler, worked with Octavia on the St. Peter's maternity ward and always liked the nights that "Bridgie" was working. She claimed Octavia had "delivered more babies than any of the doctors in Helena. When a doctor wasn't around, Mrs. Bridgwater delivered the baby." (Octavia was often called Mrs. Bridgwater, although she never married.)

Octavia was the sole Black nurse working at St. Peter's, which reportedly provided equal treatment for Black patients as well as Whites. She earned the respect of her peers, her patients, and community members. Mary Munger, former executive director of the Montana Nurses Association, stated in an article that Bridgwater was respected by her co-workers and knew what she was doing. Munger would see Octavia at Montana Nurses Association meetings in the late 1940s and 1950s. "In 1950 there were still four state nurses' associations that did not accept Black nurses into membership," Munger noted. Octavia was elected to a number of different MNA offices over the years, indicating she was respected by her peers. She was a board member of the Montana Nurses Association in 1956 and served on its public relations committee.

RACIAL DISCRIMINATION, 1930s–1960s

While Octavia was earning her nursing degree in New York at one of the only two nursing schools in the North that accepted Blacks, racism continued around the country, and in Montana. A sampling of these occurrences put Octavia's challenges in context.

Racism has early roots in Montana. "Structural racism and threats of violence toward African Americans and other people of color were pervasive throughout Montana's history," according to Montana Historical Society historian Kate Hampton. Hampton notes that "Sammy Hayes [a Black man] was killed in a riot when he tried to vote in Helena's 1867 election."

During World War I, the Black population in Helena decreased, with many of the men called into service. The decline continued. In 1920, 220 African Americans lived in Helena. By 1930, the number had dwindled to 131.

"The problems of the Great Depression affected virtually every group of Americans," reads an article on race relations in the 1930s and 1940s on the Library of Congress website. "No group was harder hit than African Americans, however. By 1932, approximately half of African Americans were out of work. In some Northern cities, Whites called for African Americans to be fired from any jobs as long as there were Whites out of work. Racial violence again became more common, especially in the South. Lynchings, which had declined to eight in 1932, surged to 28 in 1933."

Outright discrimination took place everywhere in the United States, including the nation's capital. In 1939, renowned African-American contralto Marian Anderson was denied access to perform a concert at Constitution Hall by the Daughters of the American Revolution. In response, First Lady Eleanor Roosevelt publicly resigned her membership in the DAR, and she and President Roosevelt arranged for Anderson to hold a concert on the steps of the Lincoln Memorial. It drew a crowd of 75,000.

Hampton notes that "Marian Anderson gave a wonderfully received concert in Billings in February 1938, in Great Falls in January 1947, and in Missoula in March 1956." Yet Montana had its share of discrimination. In a 1979 interview with Sally Hilander for the *Independent Record*, Norman Howard, grandson of James Crump, a pioneering Black resident in Helena, reflected on what it was like to be Black in Montana. He told the reporter that while Montana never posted signs for "Whites Only" as in the South, the same rules applied, and most Blacks found menial employment as waiters, janitors, and hotel workers. Black people were excluded from nearly every restaurant in town and held low-paying jobs, "and you'd better not go in a bar and drink,'" Howard said.

Historian Kate Hampton concurs. "During the early and mid-twentieth century," she said, "members of Montana's African American communities were denied their rights on a regular basis, from restrictions on club memberships, denial of access to public places and refusal of service to violence, threats, and criminalization of interracial marriage.

In a 2000 talk to Helena High School students about respecting diversity, Dr. Ray Howard recalled growing up in Helena and being "Helena's only Black student during the 1950s." (According to Hampton, given Helena's Black population at the time, it's likely Howard was the only Black student in his class, but not the only one among all local public schools.) An outstanding athlete, Howard played on high school teams and was president of the junior class, but he was never truly absorbed into the high school culture. As he said, "[W]hite students didn't socialize with 'colored' students. It was an unspoken rule." He was never mistreated by other students, "but I was never invited to their parties," he said.

He also told the students about vividly remembering the moment he became a "nigger." He described how he skipped excitedly to school on his first day of first grade in Billings, holding his grandmother's hand, when a crowd of White children gathered around them saying, "Look at the niggers."

Historian Ken Robison said Howard's experiences in school mirrored those of a Black classmate of Robison's, Wade Parker, in Great Falls, who was president of his senior class in the 1950s. "Yet when he walked out the doors of the school," Robison said, "he wasn't invited to the private parties, he certainly couldn't date White girls."

Howard and Parker were facing "what their parents had faced their whole lives if they were longtime Montanans," Robison said. "They could vote, they could have really decent and sometimes great experiences in school, but they couldn't join most clubs or unions. Things were separate but equal."

And in a lot of cases, not so equal.

One of the stories that's truly troubling and highlights both the racial antagonism and ambivalence in Montana comes from the life of Alma Jacobs, who was a contemporary of Octavia's and a fellow member of the Montana Federation of Colored Women's Clubs.

Robison recounted a day in the mid-1950s when Arlyne Reichert invited her friend Alma Jacobs to lunch at Schell's Townhouse in downtown Great Falls. Jacobs, who was Black and the director of the Great Falls Library, told her friend it was likely she wouldn't be admitted to the restaurant. She was right. Jacobs, who was born in Lewistown but grew up in Great Falls, had been hired as a catalog librarian in 1946 at Great Falls Library and was appointed library director in 1954. In 1973 she was hired as the Montana State Librarian. Accomplishments and contributions to the community didn't matter to those who saw only skin color.

The denial of service Jacobs encountered was an all-too-familiar scene Black people faced during the Jim Crow era in Montana. African-American U.S. Air Force personnel in Great Falls were denied entry to restaurants, bars, theaters, and even the United Service Organization (USO) Club. It's the same racism that prevented Black residents from being served in restaurants, hotels, theaters, and train and bus depots statewide, according to Hampton. Robison, in his book chapter, noted that in Helena there were a few notable exceptions where Blacks were welcomed: one Chinese restaurant, the Northern Pacific Station, and the bus depot.

Daily, casual insults must have taken an emotional toll on Octavia and others who experienced them. Despite these societal attitudes, Octavia "was nobody's victim," recalled Bonnie Bowler. She always carried herself with dignity.

Through the Pleasant Hour Club (PHC), members challenged racial discrimination in Montana and the nation. Charnan Williams wrote that the club was a "grassroots social, cultural, philanthropic, and political activist group that emphasized both self-reliance and equal opportunity for African Americans."

Club members took part in legislative lobbying and letter writing to elected officials. The PHC was a member of the Montana Federation of Colored Women's Clubs (originally called the Montana Federation of Negro Women's Clubs), which was very active politically.

Club members worked on both local and national issues, such as writing letters to support the Scottsboro Boys, who were wrongfully accused of sexual assault in 1931. In 1937, the club supported an anti-lynching campaign by the National Association for the Advancement of Colored People (NAACP) by purchasing, wearing, and selling anti-lynching buttons. They also worked against segregation practices in Montana and collaborated with the Montana Federation of Colored Women's Clubs to establish civil rights legislation in the state. Beginning in the 1930s, they wrote to the legislature, Williams noted, "urging the state to end segregation and to provide equal housing and employment opportunities for Black Montanans."

They proposed a 1937 civil rights bill that died in committee. They introduced a new bill in 1938 that would ensure fair access to public accommodations, employment, and housing. They wrote, "We are asking only the right, which we are currently denied, to live and earn an honest living as other citizens do." They encouraged others to join them in letter writing and visiting state senators and representatives.

In 1939, when Octavia was president of the club, she attempted to meet local legislative representatives about a pending civil rights bill, but none would meet with her. Club members attended the legislative session. While there were some passionate supporters of the bill, such as Representative Ben Miles, speaking in favor of passage, detractors, such as Representative R. E.

Morrison, trivialized the discrimination, comparing it to ostracism he received in grade school because of his red hair and freckles. The bill failed to pass.

Throughout the 1950s, Black women organizations proposed numerous civil rights bills to the Montana Legislature, most of which were rejected, according to Williams. From 1949 to 1955, the Montana Federation of Colored Women's Clubs (MFCWC) led the campaign to pass civil rights legislation in Montana, encountering resistance from White Montanans who claimed that there was no prejudice, and if it did exist it couldn't be legislated away.

A 1953 civil rights bill was shot down by Senator W. B. Spear, Jr., from Big Horn County. In "'Lifting as We Climb': The Activism of the Montana Federation of Colored Women's Clubs," a Montana Historical Society blog, Annie Hanshew quotes an observer of the debate, who reported that "as a Senator from a county heavily populated with Indians, [Spear said that] White constituents would expect him to defeat any legislative attempt to enforce the extension of full rights of public accommodation to the Indians," and that his failure to do so could be his political death. Similarly, a Yellowstone County legislator said he was reluctant to support the bill because of the "Mexican Problem" in his county.

Hanshew notes that in 1955 MFCWC members "recruited allies from organized labor, the Montana Farmers Union, churches, and White women's organizations," to show that segregation wasn't solely an issue for Black voters. "The bill guaranteeing 'equal accommodations in public places to all people, regardless of race, creed, or color' passed, but only after the state senate stripped the penalties for violating the law."

However, it wasn't until the passage of the federal Civil Rights Act of 1964 that racism was more fully addressed in Montana, and later in Montana's new state constitution in 1972. Interestingly enough, it was Montana senators Mike Mansfield and Lee Metcalf who played crucial roles in getting the Civil Rights Act passed in the U.S. Senate.

Discrimination was not an abstraction for Octavia but something she dealt with every day, including when she sought medical treatment at the veterans' hospital at Fort Harrison. She was denied treatment because she was a woman and she was Black. She asked a congressman to intervene. He did, and she received treatment.

The scrapbooks and family archive Octavia and Mamie carefully constructed over the decades, which filled sixty boxes, is now ensconced at the Smithsonian. It shows not only family photos and successes and achievements, but also numerous instances of racism in Montana, and, as Charnan Williams writes, Blacks standing up for "an equal chance to earn a living, and be self-supporting and respected in their communities." It's a particularly significant historical record, considering that the three Black newspapers in Montana that covered the lives and political concerns of the Black community and recorded their achievements had stopped publishing by 1911.

"I don't remember my aunt as being an outspoken advocate," said her great-niece Janet Harrell-Campbell." She lived such a life, demanding respect in a time when people were not necessarily given that, especially people of color."

Great-nephew Jules Harrell recalled the saying, "On a boat, you have singers and rowers." He said of Octavia, "She was a rower. She was more about work. She had kind of a stern disposition. She was more of a doer. She was just doing the work." A lot of it was through the Pleasant Hour Club, and much of it was behind the scenes. "She was always in conversation with power brokers," Harrell said. Mamie and Octavia earned the admiration and respect of a wide circle of people in the community by leading meaningful and full lives.

A news report on Mamie's death in 1950 spoke of her as a "highly respected Helena matron and influential member of the city's negro population, who endeared herself to all who came in contact with her."

One touching nod to Octavia appeared in an offhand, chatty column "Dicky Says:" in the June 14, 1976, *Independent Record*. The writer was driving across town and had hailed Octavia and offered her a ride. She politely declined, saying, "Gee, thanks so much, but I'd rather walk when the sun is shining."

He wrote, "She's been walking in the sunshine all her life, reaching out to touch so many people with kindness and concern. Nursing is her profession but now she is a little bit retired although she finds plenty of time to always do something for somebody. When they decide to select an all star citizen, I will cast my ballot for Octavia Bridgewater."

Octavia died on December 11, 1985, at the age of eighty-two. She was interred in the veterans' plot at Forestvale Cemetery in Helena.

CHAPTER 9

'Unlikely Warrior': Accountant Elouise Cobell

What inspires a Native American woman—an accountant and banker—to stand up to the largest government in the world, take it to court, and fight for more than thirteen years to win? It takes a special kind of courage, resilience, purpose, and most of all, compassion.

Elouise Pepion Cobell, also known as Yellow Bird Woman, a member of the Blackfeet Nation in Montana, proved to be that kind of warrior in this modern-day David versus Goliath battle.

In 1996, Cobell filed a class-action lawsuit (known as *Cobell v. Babbitt*) to prove that the U.S. government had plundered the wealth of American Indians, charging the government with mismanaging more than $100 billion in oil, timber, grazing, and other royalties. This was not a battle she sought, but once she began she wouldn't give up, despite government stonewalling, insults, destroying of evidence, government officials' flagrant contempt of court, and an army of government lawyers lined up against her. Her fight persisted for thirteen and a half years and involved 3,600 court filings, 220 days of trial, 80 published court decisions, and 10 appeals. The name of the lawsuit changed four times over the years, reflecting three different administrations and their secretaries of interior: *Cobell v. Babbitt, Cobell v. Norton, Cobell v. Kempthorne,* and *Cobell v. Salazar*.

In this image from December 2009, Elouise Cobell listens intently during a hearing of the U.S. Senate Indian Affairs Committee. PHOTOGRAPH COURTESY OF THE ASSOCIATED PRESS.

As if the court battle wasn't stressful enough, Cobell and her family were also subjected to anonymous death threats, according to author Beth Judy in her book, *Bold Women in Montana History*.

Born November 5, 1945, to Polite Pepion and Catherine DuBray Pepion at the Blackfeet Reservation hospital, Elouise was one of nine children. Her home had no electricity, central heating, or running water until she was twelve years old. Three of her siblings died in childhood: two in a car accident and one of pneumonia at two years old.

Their small ranch house along Birch Creek, about thirty miles southeast of Browning, was also home to her grandfather and several other relatives living with them. Her father served on the tribal council and was also a tribal stock inspector, making him a trusted tribal leader whom people turned to with their troubles. She grew up hearing their stories and those of her ancestors. Cobell was the great-great-granddaughter of the famous Blackfeet leader Mountain Chief, or *Ninna-stako*, who, after the 1870 Baker Massacre of Blackfeet on the Marias River, had refused any further compromises with the U.S. government.

Cobell's father also told her of how the U.S. government starved her tribe during The Starvation Winter of 1883–1884. Indian agent John Young had made sure that the Blackfeet couldn't leave their reservation, recounted Cobell in an interview with journalist Melinda Janko. Cobell said that government officials

> **would not allow Indian people to hunt or carry arms because they wanted them to be dependent on the Indian agent. And so people just hung around and waited for their rations. The rations were diverted and black-marketed, and the women and children and men had to stay confined without any means to hunt. As a result, 500 Blackfeet Indians starved to death. And the government just dug big open-pit graves and threw them in and covered it up.**

In Cobell's daily travels along U.S. Highway 89, which runs through the Blackfeet Nation, she passed by their sacred burial site, Ghost Ridge, and the historical marker. It spurred her to persist with the lawsuit even when she was exhausted. "I drive this road every single day, and some days I feel really, really tired of fighting this lawsuit against the United States government, and all I have to do is look up to the west and see Ghost Ridge, and remember all the people that starved to death for injustice. And so then it becomes their fight; it becomes the fight of the people of Ghost Ridge that we are trying to hold the United States accountable for."

Other stories Elouise heard were of missing money and the plight of tribal members unable to get the trust monies that were owed them by the federal government. The story that moved Cobell the most was that of her aunt, who needed her lease money to pay for medical care for her sick husband. "It was a harsh winter and they traveled thirty miles through snow in a horse and buggy to get to the agency office, but they wouldn't let them in," Cobell recalled in her interview with Janko.

"They waited outside in freezing cold weather all day. At the end of the day the agency told them, 'Come back tomorrow.' The next day they waited again and at the end of the day the agency told them, 'Go home.' Their check finally came in the spring. My aunt died without ever seeing justice, and her husband died from lack of medical care."

The creation of these trust funds traces back to the passage of the Allotment Act or Dawes Act in 1887, which split up millions of acres of tribal land across the country into parcels ranging in size from 40 to 320 acres that were "conveyed in trust to individual Indians." The government judged Indians as incapable of managing their own allotments, so the federal government retained the authority to issue leases on the parcels for grazing, mining, timber harvesting, and drilling for oil and gas. This was the government's attempt to assimilate Indians into White society and turn them into farmers. Monies earned from lease activities were supposed to go into Individual Indian Money (IIM) accounts, to be paid out to the account holders. But that rarely happened.

"The Bureau of Indian Affairs, which is under the Department of Interior, managed the land in trust for individual Indian members," said Cobell. The government put the IIM funds into larger trust accounts, and the Indian account holders couldn't withdraw their money without permission. For Indians to get access to this trust money was often an onerous or impossible undertaking. Indians were promised they would receive the income from the leases and use of resources, but payments on valuable land and resources often amounted to pennies.

Once the parcels had been split up under the Dawes Act, the remaining post-allotment tribal land was considered surplus by the government and was opened up for homesteading in 1889. The Dawes Act proved to be a huge land grab from the Indians. Prior to the Dawes Act, tribal lands totaled 138 million acres nationally. By 1934, American Indians had lost almost 100 million acres, much of it to non-Indian owners.

A 1915 study by the congressional Committee on Indian Affairs readily identified the pitfalls of the government's approach. The report said that the "great wealth in the form of Indian funds" (which derived from trust lands) were "an inducement to fraud, corruption, and institutional incompetence almost beyond the possibility of comprehension." Decades later, this tangle of corruption and incompetence is exactly what Cobell confronted. Congressional investigations and Cobell's lawsuit revealed the astonishing fact that the federal government never set up an accounting system for these parcels.

It's fascinating to contemplate what first guided Cobell in her career choice that would eventually put her on this historic path facing off with a monolithic, at best indifferent, and often hostile enemy.

In 1963, after graduating from high school, Cobell studied accounting and graduated from Great Falls Business College. She then studied business at Montana State University in Bozeman until she was called home to care for her dying mother. While a student, she interned at the reservation's BIA office, and "saw many people turned away when they came to the office to ask for their money."

One day, it would happen to her. Cobell attempted to withdraw money from her IIM account, asked for a statement, and was insulted by a BIA official, who told her she wouldn't understand the statement—ignoring the fact that she was trained in accounting and business.

For a while, Cobell left reservation life behind, moving to Seattle with her childhood best friend, where she worked in accounting at a television station, KING-TV. According to Beth Judy, while living there, Cobell rekindled a friendship with Alvin "Turk" Cobell, who was also from the Blackfeet Reservation and whom she had dated briefly in high school. He was working as a commercial fisherman. They married in 1969 and had a son, also named Turk. About this time, her father, Polite Pepion, retired from ranching and needed someone to take over the ranch. So in 1971, Elouise, Turk, and their son moved to the old Pepion ranch house near Birch Creek.

In 1976 (at age thirty), Elouise Cobell was hired as the Blackfeet tribal treasurer. In this role she gained a much deeper understanding of the tangled history and accounting nightmare at the BIA and U.S. Treasury Department. One of the first things she did as treasurer was to transfer the old tribal records to computers.

In an interview with journalist Peter Maas, Cobell said, "As the tribe's treasurer, I tried to get a handle on everything. I found that the BIA's investment of Blackfeet tribal trust funds was accruing negative interest. How could this be? Under the law, this money was only supposed to be invested in the safest government securities. But when I asked about this at a meeting with the BIA supervisor, he just stared at me and said, 'Why don't you learn how to read a statement?' It was so humiliating."

Much later she would find out that the BIA had taken a big chunk of Blackfeet money and loaned it to another tribe and then forgot to replace it.

It wasn't just the tribes as a whole that were being robbed and betrayed. Through her work for the tribe and helping individual tribal members, Beth Judy writes that Cobell became convinced "that the payments of money that tribal landowners received each year from the government were much smaller than they should have been." A tribal member could have rich grazing land, or several oil wells, yet the government payments amounted to a pittance. For instance, Josephine Wild Gun owned 7,000 acres of family land being leased for grazing, oil, minerals, and timber, yet she was receiving less than $1,000 per year. As Cobell tried to help tribal members look into their IIM accounts, she found the recordkeeping in a shambles and called the BIA with questions. She was told she needed to submit her questions in writing, which she did. The BIA never answered her letters. "I did spreadsheets," she told journalist Peter Maas, "and saw huge gaps where oil and gas companies that had leased out land weren't paying anything."

She later learned that different governmental agencies had looked into BIA accounting and called for changes over the decades, but these recommendations had been ignored. Through her work as Blackfeet treasurer, she traveled and met other tribal treasurers and learned that they, too, had similar troubles with landholders' accounts.

After continuing frustrations with BIA officials, Cobell and officials from other tribes began contacting congressional members and asking them to investigate and make reforms. There, they found an ally in Representative Mike Synar, an Oklahoma Democrat, who initiated an investigation in 1989. And in 1992, Congress published a report, "Misplaced Trust: The Bureau of Indian Affairs' Mismanagement of the Indian Trust Fund." The report accused BIA of malfeasance and demanded significant changes in the Department of Interior's handling of IIM and tribal trust funds. Congress passed the American Indian Trust Fund Management Reform Act of 1994 to address Department of Interior deficiencies and problems with IIM accounts.

For more than 100 years, the BIA had been collecting royalties from Indian lands and putting them into a general fund account instead of the proper individual accounts. This money was then used by the government for various purposes that didn't benefit Indians. For example, during a financial crisis in the 1970s, the federal government apparently buoyed small American banks by giving them Indian money. The total lack of any formal accounting procedures made it simple for the government and officials to misuse the money, and also to outright steal it.

Cobell also had to contend with other financial disasters. In 1983, the Blackfeet Reservation faced a crisis when the only bank on the reservation closed and no other bank was willing to step in. Businesses and services on the reservation felt the ripple effects and began closing.

Cobell went to the tribal council and proposed that the tribe found its own bank. The Blackfeet National Bank (BNB) opened its doors in 1987 and was the first national bank to be owned by a tribe. Beth Judy recounted that Cobell and tribal officials completed hundreds of thousands of pages of paperwork to create the bank, a sharp contrast to the lack of rigor the U.S.

government demonstrated in its mismanagement of its Indian trust accounts. The BNB later became Native American Bank in 2001, with a branch in Browning. Native American Bank is owned by more than thirty tribes and has expertise in loaning to Native Americans and encouraging economic development in Indian communities. Cobell would later serve as director of the Native American Community Development Corporation, which was the nonprofit affiliate of the Blackfeet Bank.

David Matheson, a member of the Coeur d'Alene Tribe and deputy commissioner of Indian Affairs at the BIA, was sympathetic to Cobell and her struggles. In 1992, he set up a meeting with Cobell and banking experts. Among them was Dennis Gingold, one of the top banking lawyers in the country. After hearing Cobell's account, he urged her to sue the government. Gingold warned her, however, that it would cost a lot of money, which the tribes did not have.

In an interview with J. Michael Kennedy, a *Los Angeles Times* reporter, Matheson said that he believed his own family had been cheated by the BIA in timber sales and land leases. He said they had been warned by the BIA to not make trouble. "The BIA had a very prominent role in generations gone by in taking resources from the tribes and giving them to other people," he said. "But then a generation would pass and the problems never got resolved. We all heard it over and over again."

Following passage of the 1994 American Indian Trust Fund Management Reform Act, President Bill Clinton appointed Paul Homan as a special trustee to ensure that the BIA complied with the new law and properly managed the accounts. A veteran banker, Homan had extensive experience in cleaning up problem banks. The BIA was directed to give him a full report of its finances and details of the accounts as far back in time as possible. But the BIA refused to follow the law and refused to cooperate with Homan. Kennedy reported that "[o]f the 238,000 individual trusts Homan's crew located, 50,000 had no addresses, which meant the money never left the Treasury. Some 16,000 accounts had no documents at all, and 118,000 were missing crucial papers." Homan said that it was likely funds had been taken from the trusts over the years. "It's akin to leaving the vault door open. You leave it open and sooner or later it's going to tempt somebody. If you don't have records and you don't have management, you don't have much." Homan later resigned, accusing Interior Secretary Bruce Babbitt of refusing to support needed reforms.

Two years after the reform act was passed, nothing had changed. At an Indian banking conference, Cobell met U.S. Attorney General Janet Reno and told her of the problems with the BIA. Reno urged her to come to Washington, D.C., to meet with her. When Cobell arrived for the meeting, a deputy attorney told her Reno wasn't available and that she shouldn't get her hopes up. Cobell was disappointed and furious.

About that time, she met with a group of officials from three federal agencies that handle Indian money: the Department of Justice, Department of Interior (which includes the BIA), and the Treasury Department. When she told them she was frustrated at the government's indifference and "lack of response," an official responded, "Why don't you just sue us?" So she did.

She didn't want to sue, she said in an interview on C-SPAN, but she saw no alternative. "It came to the point, where I just really had to draw a line in the sand and say enough is enough. Basically the United States Treasury is running a bank that is totally out of control."

On June 10, 1996, Cobell and the Native American Rights Fund filed a class-action lawsuit against the U.S. Department of Interior for the mismanagement of the Indian Trust Fund belonging to over 300,000 individual tribe members from tribes across the country. That number would swell to 500,000 during the life of the lawsuit.

"The Cobell case is about saying no longer will we tolerate this abuse," she said. "This is our money, and this is our land."

She admitted being terrified before she filed the suit. "I was just so frightened I got goosebumps all over," she said in a documentary interview. As she stood at the Lincoln Monument and looked around, all she could see were government buildings. "I thought to myself, you are taking on the United States government." She ran back to her hotel room and called a friend and said, "You know, I can't do this." Her friend responded, "Well Elouise, if you don't do it, who will?"

Not only was Cobell the lead plaintiff, but she was also a major fundraiser, tapping into relationships with organizations she'd engaged with over the years. Among them were some major foundations. Her work caught the eye of the John D. MacArthur Foundation, which awarded her a "genius" grant of $300,000 in 1997. The Lannan Foundation chipped in a reported $5 million for the fight. J. Patrick Lannan met with Cobell and said of her, "There was something about her that really impressed us. I guess it was her ability to describe what it's been like to be an Indian in this sort of thing." Cobell traveled constantly, not only to speak and raise money to fund the lawsuit, but also to keep other Indians informed about the suit.

To watch her in news interviews, such as C-SPAN, one sees why she earned respect wherever she went. In the midst of years-long battling, she was a calm, thoughtful, and steady presence with total focus on the needs of her people. "The strength you find in Elouise comes from her words, comes from her resolve, comes from the inner strength she exudes, confidence in knowing how determined she will be to fight this until it is won," said U.S. Senator Tom Daschle from South Dakota.

When asked why she filed the lawsuit, she responded, "I knew the people who [were owed] this money. They were very, very poor." She knew they would never be able to file a lawsuit on their own behalf.

Cobell expected the lawsuit to take about three years, but it was sixteen years from when it was filed until the government began sending checks. The U.S. government and "a war party of attorneys," estimated at about 100, fought it every inch of the way.

The case was assigned to U.S. District Judge Royce Lamberth, a Reagan appointee, who was a former federal prosecutor. The government refused to produce needed documents. Some had been destroyed years ago, but 162 boxes of paperwork related to the case were intentionally shredded after the trial had begun. Three months passed before government lawyers revealed the shredding to the court.

Some records were stashed on reservations. Some were in Louisiana, others were in "rat-infested warehouses in New Mexico," according to Kennedy. Lamberth also learned that the Interior Department's computer system was so bad, it was easy for hackers to set up bogus trust accounts.

In February 1999, Lamberth found Babbitt, as well as Treasury Secretary Robert Rubin and an Assistant Secretary of Indian Affairs Kevin Gover, in contempt for their failure to produce records ordered by the court and imposed fines of $600,000. Then, in December 1999, Lamberth issued a 126-page opinion against the government, calling its behavior "a shocking pattern of deception," adding, "I have never seen more egregious conduct by the federal government."

Lamberth's opinion made headlines around the world. "The entire record in this case tells the dreary story of Interior's degenerate tenure as Trustee-Delegate for the Indian trust," Lamberth noted, describing it as "a story shot through with bureaucratic blunders, flubs, goofs and foul-ups, and peppered with scandals, deception, dirty tricks and outright villainy, the end of which is nowhere in sight."

A study commissioned by the Department of Interior estimated the department's liability at $40 billion. Cobell estimated that the government owed account holders $47 billion, but a group of accountants with expertise in natural resource values estimated the amount at much more than that—$176 billion.

Despite the case's painfully slow progress, Cobell proudly stated in a 2006 C-SPAN interview, "We're winning every step of the way. . . . We are right in this case." She said the lawsuit was not about reparations or damages. "This is accounting," she said. "This is accounting for the lands—the money that has come off of the lands we own. It is not about damages. This case is actually very simple. . . . It's to compel the United States to put accounting systems in place. Can you imagine that? The United States government doesn't have an accounting system to manage our money! And then they went to court for that!"

Judge Lamberth echoed Cobell's outrage, saying that the case "serves as an appalling reminder of the evils that result when large numbers of the politically powerless are placed at the mercy of institutions engendered and controlled by a politically powerful few."

In December 2009, Cobell and her attorneys reached a $3.4-billion settlement. It was the largest monetary award for any class-action suit ever brought against the U.S. government. Out of the total, $1.5 billion was to be distributed in payments of $1,000 each to individual Indian plaintiffs across the country. Of the remainder, $60 million was earmarked for an Indian Education Scholarship fund, and $1.9 billion went into the Land Buy-Back Program that was used to purchase "fractional interests" in Indian lands allotted under the Dawes Act. Indians willing to sell their interest would receive fair market value, with payment going directly into their IIM accounts. The consolidated interests were then restored to tribal trust ownership for uses benefiting the reservation community and tribal members. In short, the plan would reverse some of the fragmentation of reservation lands that took place under the Dawes Act.

Cobell knew the settlement wouldn't please everyone. The payment was far less than even conservative estimates of what the federal government really owed, and it was much less than a "compromise" sum of $27.5 billion that Cobell had hoped for. Some Indians were unhappy to learn that they would receive only $1,000 apiece. But Cobell knew she had to be realistic. "The settlement isn't perfect," she said. "I do not think it compensates all for all the losses sustained, but I do think it is fair and it is reasonable. That is what matters: A fair resolution has been achieved."

President Barack Obama congratulates Elouise Cobell after the $3.4 billion settlement was approved.
PHOTOGRAPH BY PETE SOUZA, COURTESY OF THE WHITE HOUSE ARCHIVES.

Cobell said in a statement at that time:

We have achieved a measure of justice and financial compensation for individual Indians whose trust accounts were mismanaged by our government. Indians did not receive the full financial settlement they deserved, but we achieved the best settlement we could. This is a bittersweet victory, at best, but it will mean a great deal to the tens of thousands of impoverished Indians entitled to share in its financial fruits, as well as to the Indian youth whose dreams for a better life, including the possibility of one day attending college, can now be realized.

It's clear that she knew time was of the essence. "I felt that we were owed much more money, but this could go on for hundreds of years, and people are dying," she said, referring to the elderly claimants in the case. "They haven't gotten one cent." Extending the battle, however, would have cost millions of dollars in legal expenses with no assurance there would be a larger settlement.

Cobell said the lawsuit had been expensive, stressful, and frustrating. Each step, the U.S. government was "chewing on you," she said. Part of the chewing, it turned out, was that the government audited her taxes four years in a row. The case also robbed her of precious time with her family and time she wanted to be helping her husband run their ranch. "It's been a long process," Cobell said, "but I never, ever forgot who I was fighting for." Yet she later admitted, "I would never sue the United States government again."

In Montana alone, an estimated 33,606 beneficiaries would receive a combined total of about $87 million.

"Without Elouise Cobell's tenacity it is certain that neither compensation, nor any recognition of misdeeds, would have been forthcoming," wrote the *London Telegraph.* Senator Jon Tester echoed that sentiment, saying, "There's no doubt in my mind this would not have happened without someone like Elouise Cobell."

"I never started this case with any intentions of being a hero," Cobell said in 2009, after the settlement was reached. "I just wanted this case to give justice to people that didn't have it."

U.S. Representative Tom Cole of Oklahoma said, "We're going to be talking about Elouise Cobell the way we talk about Rosa Parks fifty years from now. She's a great American who stood up for the rights of her people and in doing that expands the rights for all Americans."

In addition to the MacArthur "genius grant," Cobell received numerous recognitions over the years. Among them were honorary degrees from Montana State University and being named the Montana Trial Lawyers Association Montana Citizen of the Year in 2011.

However, as an Indian Trust beneficiary herself, Cobell never received her own government check. The "Elouise checks" were mailed over the Christmas holidays in 2012, but Cobell had died of cancer on October 16, 2011. The Department of Interior flew flags at half-staff in her honor.

President Barack Obama called the settlement an "important step towards a sincere reconciliation" between the federal government and Indians, calling the drawn-out court battle a "stain" on the nation. He awarded Cobell the Presidential Medal of Freedom posthumously on November 22, 2016. It is the nation's highest civilian honor, "presented to individuals who have made especially meritorious contributions to the security or national interests of the United States, to world peace, or to cultural or other significant public or private endeavors."

Perhaps the greatest honor was bestowed a decade before her death when her own tribe named Cobell a warrior of the Blackfeet Nation, presenting her with an eagle feather, an honor usually reserved for U.S. military veterans.

CHAPTER 10

Truth Seeker:

Minnie Two Shoes

On a December night in 1975, on a desolate stretch of the Pine Ridge Reservation, someone shot and killed Annie Mae Aquash.

The thirty-year-old mother of two had been a leading activist in the American Indian Movement and part of the militant takeover of Wounded Knee. It was months before her body was discovered by a rancher in 1976. And twenty-eight years passed before anyone was convicted of her murder.

A group of Native American journalists were at the heart of solving the murder and digging for the truth They were warned not to continue their search and were threatened, but they kept digging. The path led places they wished it never had.

One of these truth seekers was journalist Minnie Two Shoes, an Assiniboine Sioux from the Fort Peck Reservation in Montana. She and reporter and editor Paul DeMain, an Oneida-Ojibwe from Wisconsin who was founder and editor of the *News From Indian Country* newspaper, devoted more than ten years and thousands of hours in this quest. It eventually led to the murder conviction of two men.

To understand Two Shoes and the times, one needs to step back through the decades. Born Minnie Eder on March 24, 1950, in Poplar, Montana, she lived on the Fort Peck Reservation. When she was seven years old, her family moved to Chicago as part of the Bureau of Indian Affairs Relocation Program. There, she switched schools frequently and recalled being picked on because of her name, ethnicity, and short stature. While in Chicago, her parents divorced and she was separated from her siblings.

In one of her "Red Road Home" columns in May 1999, Minnie wrote about her early life and also how she earned her name, Two Shoes. In Chicago, her family was enamored with their new "teevee" with its 14-inch screen and fascinated by shows that Minnie and her siblings found quite bizarre—" *The Three Stooges* and *I Love Lucy.* Minnie wrote, "We kept waiting for the Three Stooges' mom to come in and make them behave, and we all agreed we were glad our mom wasn't as stupid as Lucy."

Much of the column is hilarious, but Minnie also writes of her low self-esteem as a teenager. She wondered if it had to do with never seeing anyone on the "teevee" that looked like her, the one possible exception being Richard Boone, the gunslinger in "Have Gun—Will Travel," who had a dark complexion and black hair—and who would indirectly influence her future moniker.

"By the time I was in my late teens," Minnie wrote, "I was involved in Native activism and the struggles of the '70s, taking part in many an occupation, takeover, and protest for Native rights. I traveled thousands of miles for a protest march—on the way I'd hit a powwow or two—and I became well known for my hitchhiking ability."

On one such adventure, Minnie and a friend hitchhiked from Rosebud, South Dakota, to Minneapolis and arrived two hours ahead of some friends who had left Rosebud at the same time. Her friends started teasing her, calling her "Have Two Shoes, Will Travel."

"Well, the name stuck," Minnie wrote, "and I've done my best to live up to it, and so I've never stuck around town too long."

One of her longest periods of sticking around was the time she lived on the Fort Peck Reservation with her five kids from 1980 to 1997, when she wrote and worked as an editor for the *Wotanin Wowapi*, an all-woman newspaper on the reservation. In 1983 she earned a bachelor's degree in community development and a year later, in June 1984, helped found the Native American Press Association, which later became the Native American Journalists Association. Its mission was to do a better job of communicating with the estimated 1.5

Well known for her crackling sense of humor, Minnie Two Shoes pursued her education and career with serious intensity. PHOTOGRAPH COURTESY OF THE SEQUOYAH NATIONAL RESEARCH CENTER.

million Native Americans in the United States at that time, but also to ensure that American Indian journalists would write news stories about Native American issues and events, instead of having Native news coverage done solely by the mainstream press.

Minnie left the reservation from 1987 to 1990 to work on her graduate degree in journalism at the University of Missouri. She intended to go on and earn a PhD. In a January 15, 1989, *Springfield News-Leader* interview, she said, "I really want to be a teacher. I'd like to go back to Montana and teach journalism on the reservation. I want to teach people how to communicate and to recognize their potential." She also spoke of wanting to write her own history of the Native American tribes of Montana.

In 1997, Minnie took a job at the Duluth *News Tribune*, which she enjoyed but noted that she was the only person of color working there.

She moved on to become editor at *Aboriginal Voices*, a magazine published in Toronto, Ontario. As much as she loved the writing, she struggled with living in a city of 4.5 million people and rarely seeing a starry night.

From there, she moved to Minneapolis and did investigative reporting for *News From Indian Country*, a bi-monthly newspaper published in Wisconsin. "I travel extensively and I love what I'm doing," she wrote in the *Wotanin Wowapi*. "After all, I'm still living up to my name: Have Two Shoes, Will Travel."

Her passion for journalism may well have started when she became involved in the American Indian Movement (AIM) in the 1970s as their publicist and an organizer for the Wounded Knee occupation. AIM was initially founded in 1968 as an advocacy group for American Indian prisoners and to give voice to urban American Indians.

It coordinated several highly publicized protests, including the 1972 Trail of Broken Treaties caravan to Washington, D.C., the week-long occupation of the Bureau of Indian Affairs building in Washington, D.C., that year, and the seventy-one-day occupation of Wounded Knee on the Pine Ridge Reservation in South Dakota in 1973.

AIM sought to get national attention for American Indians and the economic, political, and social injustices they face. It also sought to unite Native American voices, attracting 700 activists from 200 tribes for the Trail of Broken Treaties caravan. AIM's actions were part of the rise of what became known as the Red Power movement to restore and sustain a sense of self-determination and sovereignty in Native communities. AIM's occupation at Wounded Knee called attention to poor living conditions on the reservation and the federal government's violation of treaties. It was also symbolically powerful—Wounded Knee was the site where, in 1890, the U.S. Cavalry massacred 150 Lakota men, women, and children.

AIM's occupation soon turned into an armed confrontation between AIM members and their supporters versus the Federal Bureau of Investigation, federal marshals, up to 1,000 special agents, plus the militia-like followers of a controversial Oglala tribal chairman, Richard Wilson, whose group was known as Guardians of the Oglala Nation, or GOONs.

It was, in fact, an attempt to impeach chairman Wilson and remove him from office that first drew AIM to the Pine Ridge Reservation at the invitation of a group of Oglala "traditionals." The takeover galvanized Native Americans, and many supporters traveled to the Pine Ridge Reservation to show their solidarity. The reservation quickly became a militarized zone, complete with U.S. military helicopters, snipers, a cordon of roadblocks around the town of Wounded Knee, armored personnel carriers, grenade launchers, machine guns, and contingents of National Guard personnel.

Conditions grew more tense when the government cut off electricity, water, and food supplies, although it was still winter, and blocked media from the site. A negotiated agreement to disarm was reached. Official reports said that two people were killed. The occupation is considered by many an important symbol of American Indian activism that opened a lot of hearts and minds to the oppression Native Americans were suffering. Speakers at the 25th anniversary event of Wounded Knee said that it inspired pride and hope that life could be better and more just for Native Americans.

Throughout the confrontation, the FBI spread disinformation to weaken AIM, sowing mistrust by heavily infiltrating the organization with informants, according to Montana historian and author Laura Ferguson. Many people later blamed this pervasive atmosphere of distrust and paranoia for leading to the execution of Annie Mae Pictou Aquash.

The Aquash murder investigation by DeMain, Two Shoes, and other Native journalists turned a fresh spotlight on AIM activist Leonard Peltier and called into question his claims of innocence in the 1975 murders of two FBI agents on the reservation. Many Native people and sympathizers considered the prominent AIM member a martyr, believing he had been framed. He was a cause célèbre with many high-profile supporters around the world.

Journalist Paul DeMain worked closely with Minnie to uncover the truth about the murder of Annie Mae Aquash. PHOTOGRAPH COURTESY OF TATÉ CARMICHAEL.

However, DeMain and Two Shoes found evidence that Peltier, who is serving life sentences for the FBI agents' murders, was guilty. And it was these two murders, and cover-up attempts about them, that led to the execution of Aquash.

In a March 2022 phone interview, DeMain said the search for the truth launched in 1994 when an AIM leader, Vernon Bellecourt, was confronted at a major AIM meeting in Minneapolis by an elder woman who questioned whether AIM was doing enough to help defend Peltier and asked what had happened to Aquash. Bellecourt told the crowd he didn't know and pointedly accused various Native journalists in the room of not doing their job and digging for the truth. Bellecourt was merely trying to divert attention and avoid answering the question, said DeMain. "So, we did what he wanted us to do, launch an inquiry and review of Peltier and Aquash cases—we found the truth." A group of twenty to twenty-five journalists began working on the investigation, DeMain said.

The investigation ratcheted up in 2001, when Ka-Mook Nichols, the former wife of AIM leader Dennis Banks, met with DeMain and confirmed that what he had been digging up and publishing in his news stories in *News From Indian Country* was accurate. Nichols told him that she and Aquash were traveling in Marlon Brando's motor home, which had been loaned to AIM leaders, and that Peltier had reenacted his close-range shooting of the agents. "Annie Mae was executed about three weeks later, when AIM security caught up with her in Denver," wrote DeMain in an email.

DeMain and Two Shoes followed up and interviewed multiple sources who had "heard Peltier brag about killing the two FBI agents," and who confirmed Peltier had reenacted the murder scene in front of Aquash, Ka-Mook Nichols, and Bernie Nichols (Lafferty), then-partner to AIM activist Bob Robideau.

From 1996 through 1998, DeMain and Two Shoes traveled to Washington, D.C., and reviewed thousands of files. "We went to the Minnesota Historical Society and reviewed tons of documents . . . 77,000 files in Washington, D.C., and a couple hundred thousand files in Minnesota," DeMain later said in a film documentary. He credited Two Shoes' excellent memory as an asset in the research and investigation, saying, "Two Shoes could remember specific dates or places, which provided beneficial evidence." He added that "Two Shoes' humor allowed her to connect with people emotionally," which proved extremely helpful as they set out to interview sixty to seventy people who might be able to confirm details in the case.

"Shoes was the inside person who had been everywhere AIM [was] from 1968–75 or so," DeMain wrote in an email. [W]hen we hit the street—[it] didn't take more than weeks to bear fruit." Both of them were so familiar with the documents and any available film footage that they were quickly able to determine if a witness was lying to them, said DeMain.

The FBI did "snitch jacketing" of Annie Mae, which was an FBI tactic—making other people believe that the target is an informer, said DeMain in a 1999 "Native America Calling" radio interview with Harlan McKosato. At least three FBI informants interacted with Aquash in the months leading up to her death, yet instead of suspicion falling on any of them, it all focused on Aquash. "The FBI was using her as a beacon, following her around in order to track leadership people," said DeMain. Suspicions were aroused because she would be picked up by authorities and released but not charged and not deported to her home country of Canada.

On the same radio call-in program, radio host Harlan McKosato asked Two Shoes why, after twenty-four years, Aquash's death was still an issue in Indian Country. She replied, "Part of why she was so important is because she was very symbolic, she was a hard-working woman, she dedicated her life to the movement, to righting all the injustices that she could. . . ."

Two Shoes then criticized the government's pervasive counterintelligence program or COINTELPRO for "bad jacketing" Aquash to such a point that she was murdered. "(Y)ou gotta remember that it was mostly women in AIM. It could have been any one of us, and I think that's why it's been so important, and she was just such a good person."

Two Shoes might very well have seen her own possible fate in that of Aquash's. Two Shoes had her own chilling encounter and interrogation by AIM leaders at a 1975 "liberation" of the Alexian Brothers' Novitiate abbey in Wisconsin, when she and her husband, John Carmichael, were treated like they were informers. They were directed to go upstairs to a room crammed with people, including AIM leaders Dennis Banks, Leonard Peltier, Herb Powless, Theda Nelson Clarke, and others.

They were told there was a lot of talk about Two Shoes' husband being an informant. In response, Carmichael made a sarcastic facial expression. Powless responded, "If I were you, I'd take that smirk off your face, we can arrange to wipe that smirk off, you know." Two Shoes and her husband were then escorted to their car and told to leave.

This incident was particularly haunting when decades later Two Shoes shared the story with Iris Thunder Cloud, who had traveled to an AIM conference in New Mexico with Aquash in 1975. While Thunder Cloud and Aquash were in their tent that night, AIM leaders came and took Aquash away for hours.

As Two Shoes recounted in testimony published in *News From Indian Country* in February 2002, "Anna Mae told her [Thunder Cloud] that the three men had questioned her about being an informer and that Leonard Peltier put a gun in her mouth and asked her if she was a spy for the government. Anna Mae 'was shaking and started crying' and she questioned why AIM was doing that to her," Thunder Cloud told Two Shoes. A few months later, Aquash disappeared.

In 2002, DeMain began publishing evidence that Aquash and several other people were witnesses to an incriminating event: Peltier's reenactment of the 1975 murder of two FBI agents. Others in AIM decided they needed to do something about it—to make sure Aquash never talked. However, there has never been any evidence that Aquash was ever a government informant. In fact, the FBI publicly denied that she was an informant.

While DeMain and Two Shoes dug for facts, they faced threats. "We were told to be careful by far too many people, hollered at, sent death threats by weird phone calls," recounted DeMain in an email. "[Yakama journalist Richard] LaCourse found a hand gun, sitting on his outdoor window sill, when he had been working on some of this . . . and we did extra security about where we went, and who knew what, but I don't think it impressed Minnie at all—pissed her off, and she went where she wanted to and said things to Dennis Banks, Vernon and Clyde Bellecourt—all of them—whenever she wanted."

By the time they were done digging, DeMain said, "we had upturned at least a dozen alleged murders perpetrated by AIM members, including Black civil rights worker Perry Ray Robinson, Jr., Penobscot Johnnie Moore, and Jeanette Bisonette of Pine Ridge, all killed because of accusations involving being informants. And I doubt they were the only ones."

In a 2022 telephone interview, DeMain said, "I was told by a well-known AIM member from Green Bay, Wisconsin, that a contract was allegedly taken out on my life . . . by Minneapolis AIM. Some of it was just scare tactics and bully tactics . . . but there were scary and dangerous people."

Two men were eventually convicted of Aquash's murder, Arlo Looking Cloud in 2004 and John Graham in 2010. Both had worked AIM security in the past. Graham is serving a life sentence in a South Dakota state prison. Looking Cloud was convicted and sentenced to life in prison in federal court, but received a sentence reduction because of his own admission to involvement in the case. He was released on parole in 2020. No one in AIM leadership was ever charged with ordering the killing, even though Russell Means, in a 1994 press conference, accused two other AIM leaders of ordering Aquash's murder.

DeMain said he believes that there was a collective decision "that there was a problem that needed to be gotten rid of." Word got out on the street that something needed to be done about it.

DeMain commented in news stories that he found it interesting "that it has been the women—including the late journalist Minnie Two Shoes and AIM-member-turned-government-witness Ka-Mook Banks," who kept asking questions about what happened to Aquash, even when they didn't like the answers. "I've found that the courageous people have been the women in the American Indian Movement," DeMain said.

Two Shoes' courage was evident even before this time. She had been a firm supporter of AIM's goals. Their motto, "Anywhere Anytime Anyplace," referred to their willingness to confront inequalities, except, it seems, their own. As student journalist Sada Schumann says, Minnie "found the group and its leaders refused to acknowledge the injustice within the group, particularly the clear patriarchy preventing any woman from taking on a leadership role."

"She criticized male AIM members who got drunk, slept around, and fathered children they did not raise," wrote Laura Ferguson. Minnie's challenging comments, plus the unfounded accusations against her that she was an FBI informer, resulted in her expulsion from AIM.

"Minnie talked a lot about the sexism and misogynistic stuff," said DeMain, and said she was particularly upset with an AIM leader who fathered numerous children with many women, but was not paying child support and was not challenged for his behavior. "Minnie was American Indian Movement no matter who said she could or couldn't be," said DeMain. "Minnie was the epitome of the American Indian Movement's revival of language and custom, the revival of singing and dancing and heritage—of all that stuff." In 1980, Two Shoes started a women's traditional society on the Fort Peck Reservation.

The dramatic murder investigation and exposé are but part of the life story of this fascinating and fearless activist. Minnie Two Shoes was known for her honesty and courage in standing up to hypocrisy, sexism, and corruption wherever she found them.

A case in point was when Two Shoes had been promised a permanent slot as an associate editor at the *Wotanin Wowapi* on the Fort Peck Reservation. But when she wrote an article that a tribal council member with inside information had won all the tribal contracts for new HUD housing on the reservation, "the council voted someone else to the job," she said at a Native American Press Association (NAPA) conference.

This was but one example of why she and other American Indian journalists got together in 1983 to establish NAPA, which would later become the Native American Journalists Association (NAJA), to protect freedom of the press for reservation newspapers and other reservation news outlets. These were often the only news organizations covering stories on reservations, and typically their funding was controlled by tribal officials. Native journalists found that on reservations, they didn't have legal protections for freedom of the press.

She inspired a new generation of journalists by teaching them techniques of storytelling that conveyed a deeper message, said Ferguson. "She mentored and took them in the field so that they could get some actual experience. She brought her humor into that. She told them it's okay to tell a serious story and bring humor into it because humor humanizes people."

Among the many stories Two Shoes wrote were those about child abuse hurting everyone, and also, as Ferguson noted, articles about "safe houses

Minnie Two Shoes, far left, stands with colleagues at the Native Media Awards in 2003. PHOTOGRAPH COURTESY OF TATÉ CARMICHAEL.

for domestic violence victims, environmental contamination on reservations, and the high rates of cancer-related deaths among American Indian women." Ironically, Minnie would be one of those women killed by cancer on April 9, 2010.

"She was a good writer, a good historian. She wrote good stories about good things," said DeMain. In 2009, NAJA honored Two Shoes with an award for journalistic excellence.

"As journalists, we're very special people," said Two Shoes, "and we have a very serious responsibility—but that doesn't mean we can't have fun along the way." According to a number of accounts, there was no shortage of fun when Two Shoes showed up. She and the "*Wotani* girls" were renowned for their ability to swoop in on the journalism conference's delectable food, and "an awful lot of good food ended up in their rooms," which they would then generously share with others, said DeMain.

Minnie and DeMain also liked to share the wealth of food with homeless people. He recalled several conferences where he and Two Shoes wrapped up large amounts of conference food that would have been discarded and, sometimes using a tablecloth to secure it, hauled it out to homeless folks on the streets and living under bridges.

Two Shoes was well known for her flamboyant personality, her off-beat jokes, her commitment to the truth, and, of course, her must-read, award-winning newspaper column, "Red Road Home." One delightful column discussed at length the quest for the perfect Indian taco and how one chooses just the right taco stand. Folks tend to rely on gossip, plus advice from their grannies, their friends, and uncles and cousins as well as noting the amount of foot traffic a taco stand is drawing—and what the taco looks like on the plates that are passing by—before they make their perfect taco purchase.

She urged tribal members to use the same care and level of scrutiny to examine their tribal council candidates before voting or they might wind up with "a bad taste in [their] mouth."

Two Shoes also wrote about her Rez Bomb, noting that she drove it "for the sake of recycling." As Ferguson recounted, Minnie wrote, "That's what I tell my kids when they ask why the cars on the reservation are older models. . . . We're using up our cars all the way, like the old Indians did with the buffalo."

There were so many noteworthy Rez Bombs on the reservation that *Wotanin Wowapi* editor Bonnie Red Elk and assistant editor Two Shoes held an annual contest for "Ugliest Car on the Reservation."

National columnist Tim Giago, who founded *Indian Country Today*, wrote in a 2006 column, "The Ugliest Car on the Reservation," that the contest was much anticipated at his newspaper. "Whenever their newspaper arrived at my office with the winner, my staff and I would hold our sides in pain from laughing so hard," Giago wrote. "There were so many ugly cars entered in the contest that unbiased judges had a heck of a time selecting the winner."

"She was one of those people that the younger journalists gravitated to," recalled Daniel Littlefield, director of the Sequoyah National Research Center, which has the world's largest archived collection of Native American newspapers and other publications. He remembered young journalists seeking her out at NAJA meetings. From early on, NAJA grew out of Native American activism at Alcatraz, Wounded Knee, and Trail of Broken Treaties. "Those actions caused the tribes to realize that they needed to be writing the news rather than having mainstream reporters do that," Littlefield said. "That's why we needed to archive the words of Native people. Who's going to write the history fifty years from now?"

Littlefield predicted, "I think she's going to be an icon" in the indigenous journalism world that people will hold up and say, "what she was doing is what we should be doing."

While recovering in Florida during a bout with breast cancer in 2004, Two Shoes wrote an open letter to the *Wotanin Wowapi* titled, "Where is Minnie Two Shoes?" She spoke a bit about herself. "A friend told me in the days just after the 1973 liberation of Wounded Knee in South Dakota that I was 'painfully honest and excruciatingly sincere.' I've tried all my life to walk in balance and that will sometimes explain my wild zigs and zags in my career and personal life." She also reflected on being a grandma: "Take action to make sure that Mother Earth remains here forever—IN GOOD SHAPE—not only for the creatures we share our home with but for the coming generations. Without her we are nothing."

Upon Two Shoes' death from cancer, NAJA President Ronnie Washines wrote, "She was a sincere advocate of free press, free speech and free food for everyone. She held a deep respect and love for NAJA and the mission of the organization."

In 2009, when Two Shoes received her NAJA award, she told a student journalist during an interview, "It makes me realize, that as part of what years ago we said we wanted, was to create journalists to come and take our place. . . . Well," she joked, "I've got some really tiny shoes to fill."

Of the many moving tributes made about Two Shoes, historian Laura Ferguson highlighted one by NAJA member Deborah Locke, who said, "When Minnie entered any room in the world, laughter walked in with her, sat down, and stayed." ~

Sources

CHAPTER 1—HUM FAY

- Bakken, Gordon Morris, and Alexandra Kindell. *Encyclopedia of Immigration and Migration in the American West*, Vol. 1. Sage Publishing, 2006.
- Baumler, Ellen. "Driving the Golden Spike." *Great Falls Tribune*, March 21, 2015.
- *Butte Bystander.* Silver Bow Trades and Labor Assembly, February 11, 1893
- "Butte Chinese are Divided on Cues." *Anaconda Standard*, February 5, 1911.
- The *Butte Miner*, March 24, 1912.
- Drake, Phil. "A Life Through Letters: Book Looks at Chinese Experience in Montana." Helena *Independent Record*, May 22, 2022.
- Flaherty, Stacy A. "Boycott in Butte: Organized Labor and the Chinese Community, 1896–1897." *Montana, The Magazine of Western History*, Vol. 37. No. 1 (Winter 1987).
- "Hum Fay." Mai Wah Museum, Butte, Montana. https://www.maiwah.org/explore/butte-chinese-experience/hum-fay/. Accessed March 11, 2022.
- Johnson, Mark T. *The Middle Kingdom Under the Big Sky: A History of the Chinese Experience in Montana*. University of Nebraska Press, 2022.
- Luo, Michael. "The Forgotten History of the Purging of Chinese from America." *The New Yorker*, April 22, 2021.
- Merritt, Christopher William. "The Coming Man From Canton: Chinese Experience in Montana (1862–1943)." PhD dissertation, University of Montana-Missoula, 2010.
- *Montana Standard.* "Pauper's Grave Will Claim Body of Chinese 'Big Shot' in Halcyon Days of Butte." April 22, 1932.
- Strandberg, Greg. "A History of Montana's Early Chinese." Big Sky Words blog. www.bigskywords.com/montana-blog/a-history-of-montanas-early-chinese.
- Swartout, Jr., Robert R. "From Guangdong to the Big Sky: The Chinese Experience in Frontier Montana, 1864–1900, in *Montana: A Cultural Medley*, Robert R. Swartout, Jr., ed. Farcountry Press, 2015.

- Swartout, Jr., Robert R. "Kwantgtung to Big Sky: The Chinese in Montana, 1864–1900." *A Chinese on the American Frontier*. Arlif Dirlik, ed. Lanham: Rowman & Littlefield, 2001.
- Testimony from Hum Fay. *Hum Fay, et al. vs. Baldwin, et al.* Records, 1898. Manuscript Collection 43 [box 1 folder 3]. Montana Historical Society Research Center Archives. Reprinted in Chapter 15, *Montana: Stories of the Land,* Krys Holmes, ed., Montana Historical Society Press, 2009.
- "Wedding of Chinese Belle and Butte Merchant to Be a Real Swell Affair." Butte *Daily Post*, January 15, 1909.
- Wu, Ting-Fang. Letter requesting $500,000 in damages, in Papers Relating to the Foreign Relations of the United States with the Annual Message of the President Transmitted to Congress December 3, 1901, Correspondence: Mr. Wu to Mr. Hill. https://history.state.gov/historicaldocuments/frus1901/d89.
- Wunder, John R. "Law and Chinese in Frontier Montana." *Montana, The Magazine of Western History*, Vol. 30, No. 3 (July 1980).

CHAPTER 2—CHARLES L. CRUM

- "Disloyal Miner Deported from Carpenter Creek." *Roundup Record*, May 3, 1918.
- "Ex-Judge Crum Back in Forsyth Lays His Trouble to Political Frame-up—Will Open Law Office." *Roundup Record*, January 29, 1919.
- "Force Pro-Germans to Swear Allegiance and Burn German Books." *Roundup Record*, March 29, 1918.
- Gutfeld, Arnon. "'Stark, Staring, Raving Mad': An Analysis of a World War I Impeachment Trial." *Yearbook of German-American Studies*, Vol. 30, 1995.
- Holmes, Krys. *Montana: Stories of the Land*. Montana Historical Society Press, 2009.
- Iwanski, Len. "Senate Clears Former Judge." *Great Falls Tribune*, January 27, 1991.
- Kennedy, David M. *Over Here: The First World War and American Society, Twenty-fifth Anniversary Edition*. Oxford University Press, 2004.
- Montana Council on Defense. "Orders of the Montana Council on Defense." See the file on Judge Charles Crum at the Montana Historical Society.
- "Montana Judge Flees Country." *Sanders County Independent Ledger*, March 28, 1918.

- Montana Legislature, Senate Judiciary Committee. "Statement of David A. Walter." *Hearing before the Senate Judiciary Committee on Senate Resolution 2—A Resolution to Exonerate Charles Liebert Crum.* January 25, 1991. Montana Historical Society Vertical File Charles L. Crum.
- Montana Legislature, "Statement of Darwin Crum." January 25, 1991. Montana Historical Society Vertical File Charles L. Crum.
- Robison, Ken. *World War I Montana: The Treasure State Prepares.* The History Press, 2018.
- Sauer, Patrick. "World War: 100 Years Later, The Year Montana Rounded Up Citizens for Shooting Off Their Mouths." *Smithsonian.com Special Report*, January 14, 2015. www.smithsonianmag.com/history/year-montana-rounded-citizens-shooting-their-mouths-180953876/. Accessed October 17, 2018.
- "Says Judge Crum Opposed Draft." Spokane *Spokesman Review*, February 23, 1918.
- *State of Montana Proceedings of the Court for the Trial of Impeachments: The People of the State of Montana By the House of Representatives Thereof Against Charles L. Crum, Judge of the Fifteenth Judicial District of the State of Montana.* State Publishing Company, 1918.
- Walter, Dave. "Casualties of War: The Tragedy of Judge C. L. Crum." *Montana Magazine*, Vol. 104 (November–December 1990).
- Walter, Dave. "Impeaching Judge Crum." *Montana Campfire Tales: Fourteen Historical Narratives*, TwoDot Books, 1997.
- Work, Clemens P. *Darkest Before Dawn: Sedition and Free Speech in the American West.* University of New Mexico Press, 2005.

CHAPTER 3—GEORGE M. BOURQUIN

- Bailey, C. H. "Bourquin Human in Court and Out: Even Those He Sentences Like Him." *Judith Basin Star*, March 1925, reprint of article that originally appeared in the San Francisco *Bulletin*, no date.
- "Bar Association Defends Bourquin." *Anaconda Standard*, February 24, 1918.
- Gutfeld, Arnon. "George Bourquin: A Montana Judge's Stand Against 'Government Despotism.'" *Western Legal History*, Vol. VI, No, 1, Winter/Spring 1993.
- Gutfeld, Arnon. *Montana's Agony: Years of War and Hysteria, 1917–21.* University Press of Florida, 1979.

- Gutfeld, Arnon. "'Stark, Staring, Raving Mad': An Analysis of a World War I Impeachment Trial." *Yearbook of German-American Studies,* Vol. 30, 1995.
- Gutfeld, Arnon. *Treasure State Justice: Judge George M. Bourquin, Defender of the Rule of Law.* Texas Tech University Press, 2013.
- Gutfeld, Arnon. "Western Justice and the Rule of Law: Bourquin on Loyalty, the 'Red Scare,' and Indians." *Pacific Historical Review,* Vol. LXV, No. 1, February 1996.
- Inbody, Kristen. "Montana Judge Stands Strong for Free Speech." *Great Falls Tribune,* March 9, 2014.
- Jameson, William J. Letter from U.S. Senior District Court Judge to Chet Orloff, Executive Director, 9th Judicial Circuit Historical Society. Pasadena, California, October 22, 1987.
- Johnson, Charles F. "78 Convicted of Sedition in Montana Pardoned: Anti-German Hysteria During WWI Put Many in Prison." *Billings Gazette,* May 3, 2006.
- "Judge Bourquin Holds Hall and Just Not Liable." Helena *Independent Record,* January 27, 1918.
- "Judge Bourquin, Montana Federal Jurist 22 Years, Summoned at 95." Butte *Montana Standard,* November 17, 1958.
- "Memory of U.S. Judge George M. Bourquin Honored With Eulogy." Butte *Montana Standard,* January 6, 1959.
- Renz, Jeffrey, and Clemens P. Work. Letter to Governor Brian Schweitzer, March 27, 2006.
- Robbins, Jim. "Pardons Granted After 88 Years After Crimes of Sedition." *The New York Times,* May 3, 2006.
- Toole, K. Ross. *Twentieth-Century Montana: A State of Extremes.* University of Oklahoma Press, 1972.
- Walter, Dave. "Patriots Gone Berserk: The Montana Council of Defense, 1917–1918." *More Montana Campfire Tales.* Farcountry Press, 2002.
- Work, Clemens P. *Darkest Before Dawn.* University of New Mexico Press, 2005.

CHAPTER 4—JOHN FRANZ

- Dick, LaVernae J. "A Noose for the Minister." *The Mennonite,* Vol. 79, April 21, 1964.

- Franz, Rufus M. "It Happened in Montana." *Mennonite Life*, October 1952.
- Inbody, Kristen. "World War I Resonates in Montana a Century Later." *Great Falls Tribune*, April 5, 2017.
- Malone, Michael P., et al. *Montana: A History of Two Centuries*. University of Washington Press, 2001.
- Mullet, Cindy. "Glendive Pastor Nearly Lynched in 1918 Because of German Ties." Glendive *Ranger Review*, November 22, 2001.
- Stoltzfus, Duane C. S. *Pacifists in Chains*. Johns Hopkins University Press, 2013.
- Stoltzfus, Duane C. S. "Standing in Chains at Alcatraz: When Hutterites Were Called to War." *The Mennonite*, August 1, 2012.
- Walter, Dave. "Patriots Gone Berserk, The Montana Council of Defense, 1917–1918." *More Montana Campfire Tales*. Farcountry Press, 2002.

CHAPTER 5—HAZEL HUNKINS

- "6 More Suffrage Pickets Arrested." *Oakland Tribune*, June 26, 1917.
- "19th Amendment to the U.S. Constitution: Women's Right to Vote (1920)." National Archives. https://www.archives.gov/milestone-documents/19th-amendment.
- "Another 'Lady from Montana.'" Helena *Independent*, June 29, 1917.
- "Centuries of Citizenship: A Constitutional Timeline, 1907–1930." The National Constitution Center. https://constitutioncenter.org/timeline/html/cw08_12159.html.
- Cimons, Marlene. "Looking Back with American's Last Suffragette." *Los Angeles Times* story reprinted in *San Francisco Chronicle*, February 5, 1980.
- "Cupid Thins Ranks: Militants of Alice Paul's Once Famous Picket Brigade Now Honeymooning." *Burlington Free Press and Times*, February 2, 1922.
- Ferris, Ruth. "Lesson Plan: Hazel Hunkins, Billings Suffragist: A Primary Source Investigation." Montana Historical Society. https://mhs.mt.gov/education/Women/HHLessonPlanFinal2.pdf. Accessed March 18, 2021.
- "Hallinan, Hazel H." Biography, Social Networks and Archival Context (SNAC), from the guide to the Papers, 1864-1984, Schlesinger Library, Radcliffe Institute. https://snaccooperative.org/ark:/99166/w66q59sv. Accessed May 5, 2021.

- "Hazel W. Hallinan, 91, Journalist and Activist." Obituary, *The New York Times*, May 19, 1982.
- Hunkins-Hallinan, Hazel, editor. *In Her Own Right: A Discussion Conducted by the Six Point Group*. George G. Harrap & Co. LTD, London, 1968.
- Hunkins, Hazel. Letter to her mother, March 30, 1917. Copy of Hunkins' typewritten letter. See Ferris, Ruth. Hazel Hunkins Lesson Plan, Montana Historical Society.
- Hunkins, Hazel. Letter to her mother, July 5, 1917. In Kevin Kooistra, "Continuing the Fight for Women's Rights: Hazel Hunkins Hallinan of Billings," Western Heritage Center, Billings.
- Hunkins, Hazel. Letter to her mother, July 8, 1917. Hazel Hunkins-Hallinan Papers, MC 532, box 61, folder 9, Schlesinger Library, Radcliffe Institute.
- Kelly, Harry. "Met by Carter: 1913 Suffragette Leads ERA March," *Chicago Tribune*, August 27, 1977.
- Kooistra, Kevin. "Civil Rights Activist Hazel Hunkins Hallinan." C-Span video library of American History TV, September 9, 2013. https://www.c-span.org/video/?315345-1/civil-rights-activist-hazel-hunkins-hallinan.
- Kooistra, Kevin. "Continuing the Fight for Women's Rights: Hazel Hunkins Hallinan of Billings." PowerPoint, Western Heritage Center, Billings, Montana.
- Kooistra, Kevin. Phone interview, March 25, 2021.
- Lange, Allison. "Women's Rights in the Early Republic." National Women's History Museum, 2015. http://www.crusadeforthevote.org/early-republic.
- McArdle, Terence. "Night of Terror: The Suffragists Who Were Beaten and Tortured for Seeking the Vote." *Washington Post*, November 10, 2017.
- "Miss Hunkins Wins in Declamatory: Will Represent Billings High School at Missoula." *Billings Gazette*, May 8, 1908.
- National Park Service. "National Woman's Party Protests During World War I." Belmont-Paul Women's Equality National Monument, National Mall and Memorial Parks, President's Park (White House). https://www.nps.gov/articles/national-womans-party-protests-world-war-i.htm. Accessed April 29, 2021.
- Olp, Susan. "Billings Woman Fought on the Front Lines for Women's Suffrage in 1910s." *Billings Gazette*, July 3, 2017.

- Pruitt, Sarah. "The Night of Terror: When Suffragists Were Imprisoned and Tortured in 1917." History.com. https//www.history.com/news/night-terror-brutally-suffragists-19th-amendment.
- Public Broadcasting Service. "Wilson and Women's Suffrage." *American Experience.* https://www.pbs.org/wgbh/americanexperience/features/wilson-womens-suffrage/.
- Roden, Jessica. "Biography of Hazel Hunkins Hallinan, 1890–1982. Introduction to Part 1: Militant Women Suffragists—National Woman's Party Biographical Database, Militant Woman Suffragists, 1913–1920." https://documents.alexanderstreet.com/d/1009554983.
- Schmidt, Samantha. "Battle for the Ballot: Thousands of women fought against the right to vote. Their reasons still resonate today." *Washington Post,* August 9, 2020.
- Social Networks and Archival Context (SNAC). "Hallinan, Hazel H." From the guide to the Papers, 1864–1984, Schlesinger Library, Radcliffe Institute. https://snaccooperative.org/view/28897674.
- "Suffragist Uses AERO." *Santa Ana Register,* September 26, 1916.
- Waters, George B. "Where Are the Suffragettes?" Honolulu *Star Bulletin,* December 6, 1920.
- "Woman Led Mob Attacking Pickets: Banners About the White House Taken from the 'Suffs' and Torn to Pieces This Afternoon." *Fort Wayne News,* June 21, 1917.

CHAPTER 6—ROBERT YELLOWTAIL

- Benson, Megan. "The Fight for Crow Water, Part 1: The Early Reservation Years." *Montana: The Magazine of Western History.* Vol. 57, No. 4, Winter 2007.
- Benson, Megan. "The Fight for Crow Water, Part 2: Damming the Bighorn." *Montana: The Magazine of Western History.* Vol. 58, No. 1, Spring 2008.
- Bernardis, Tim. Personal phone conversations, May 2020 and spring 2022; Email July 26, 2022.
- Bradley, Jr., Charles Crane, and Susanna Remple Bradley. "From Individualism to Bureaucracy: Documents on the Crow Indians 1920–1945." Unpublished pdf, 1974.
- Brooke, William M. "Yellowtail Dam: A Study in Indian Lands." Senior honors thesis, Carroll College, Helena, Montana, 1984.

- Calendar No. 183. 66th Congress 1st Session Senate Report No. 219, Crow Tribe of Indians of Montana (September 23, 1919).
- Clark, William. *Journals of the Lewis and Clark Expedition*. Clark, August 3, 1806. Center for Digital Research in the Humanities and the University of Nebraska Press. https://lewisandclarkjournals.unl.edu/item/lc.jrn.1806-08-03#lc.jrn.1806-08-03.03.
- Crum, Steven. "Crow Warrior: Robert Yellowtail Was a Life-long Advocate of Native American Higher Education." *Tribal College Journal of American Indian Higher Education,* Vol. 1, No. 4 (Spring 1990).
- Crutchfield, James A., Candy Moulton, and Terry Del Bene. *The Settlement of America: An Encyclopedia of Westward Expansion from Jamestown to the Closing of the Frontier.* Routledge, 2011.
- Edlefsen, David. "How the West was Claimed: The Homestead Act and the General Allotment Act." Prepared for Western Political Science Conference, San Francisco, CA, March 31, 2018.
- Grande, Sandy. *Red Pedagogy: Native American Social and Political Thought.* Rowman & Littlefield, 2015.
- Hoxie, Frederick E. *Indians of North America: The Crow.* Chelsea House Publishers, 1989.
- Hoxie, Frederick, and Tim Bernardis. "Robert Yellowtail: Crow." *The New Warriors: Native American Leaders Since 1900.* Edmunds, R. David, editor. Bison Books, University of Nebraska, 2004.
- Otis, D. S. *The Dawes Act and the Allotment of Indian Lands.* University of Oklahoma Press, 1973.
- Poten, Constance. "Robert Yellowtail, the New Warrior." *Montana: The Magazine of Western History.* Vol. 39, No. 3, Summer 1989.
- Sandweiss, Martha A., Carol A. O'Connor, and Clyde A. Milner II. *The Oxford History of the American West.* Oxford University Press, 1994.
- Schultz, Jeffrey D., Andrew L. Aoki, Kerry L. Haynie, and Anne M. McCulloch, eds. *Encyclopedia of Minorities in American Politics: Volume 2 Hispanic Americans and Native Americans.* Greenwood Publishing Group, 2000.
- Yellowtail, Robert S. Address before the Senate Committee on Indian Affairs, September 9, 1919. Transcription in "Toward a More Perfect Union in an Age of Diversity: American Beliefs about Equality." Public Broadcasting System. https://www.pbs.org/ampu/equality.html. Accessed February 22. 2022.

- Yellowtail, Sr., Robert Summers. *Robert Summers Yellowtail, Sr., at Crow Fair, 1972.* Wowapi/Black Jack, distributed by Cold Type Services of New Mexico, 1973.

CHAPTER 7—SUSIE WALKING BEAR YELLOWTAIL

- Askins, Kathryn A. "Bridging Cultures: American Indian Students at the Northfield Mount Hermon School." Doctoral dissertation, University of New Hampshire, 2009. https://scholars.unh.edu/dissertation/467.
- "Big Heart." Profile of Susie Walking Bear Yellowtail in *The Chronicle of Nursing,* American Society of Registered Nurses, November 1, 2007. https://www.asrn.org/journal-chronicle-nursing/205-big-heart.html.
- Bowen, Holly. "Understanding the Wagon Wheel of Life." *Moscow-Pullman Daily News,* September 13, 2011.
- Ferguson, Laura. "Susie Walking Bear Yellowtail: Our Bright Morning Star." In *Beyond Schoolmarms and Madams: Montana Women's Stories.* Martha Kohl, ed. Montana Historical Society Press, 2016.
- Gorzalka, Ann. "Memorial to Susie Yellowtail." *Country Journal,* January 6, 1982. Montana Historical Society vertical file.
- Kluchin, Rebecca. *Fit to Be Tied: Sterilization and Reproductive Rights in America, 1950–1980.* Rutgers University Press, 2009.
- Ko, Lisa. "Reproductive Rights: Unwanted Sterilization and Eugenics Programs in the United States." In *Beyond the Films,* Public Broadcasting System, January 29, 2016. https://www.pbs.org/independentlens/blog/unwanted-sterilization-and-eugenics-programs-in-the-united-states/.
- Medicine Crow, Joe. Hand-typed statement, apparently made at time of Susie Yellowtail's death. PDF 4336, Montana Historical Society vertical file.
- "Mrs. Yellowtail's Work Takes Her All Over the World." *The Sheridan Press,* July 28, 1969.
- Powell, Father Peter J. "Susie Yellowtail (1903–1981)." Appears to be a eulogy but not labeled as such. Montana Historical Society vertical file.
- "Religious Crimes Code of 1883 bans Native dances, ceremonies." In Investing in Native Communities, a joint project of Native Americans in Philanthropy and Candid. https://nativephilanthropy.candid.org/events/religious-crimes-code-of-1883-bans-native-dances-ceremonies/.

- Theobald, Brianna. "Nurse, Mother, Midwife: Susie Walking Bear Yellowtail and the Struggle for Crow Women's Reproductive Autonomy." *Montana, The Magazine of Western History*, Vol. 66, No. 3, Autumn 2016.
- Theobald, Brianna. *Reproduction on the Reservation: Pregnancy, Childbirth, and Colonialism in the Long Twentieth Century.* University of North Carolina Press, 2019.
- Theobald, Brianna. "Susie Walking Bear Yellowtail and Histories of Native American Nursing." Nursing CLIO. https://NursingCLIO.org. Accessed November 19, 2020.
- Walter, Dave. "Susie Yellowtail (1903–1981)." Montana Historical Society pdf, 1987. https://mhs.mt.gov/education/Montanans/yellowtail2.pdf.

CHAPTER 8—OCTAVIA BRIDGWATER

- "African American Nurses in World War II." National Women's History Museum, July 8, 2019. https://www.womenshistory.org/articles/african-american-nurses-world-war-ii. Accessed May 7, 2022.
- Baumler, Ellen. "Contributions of a Mother and Daughter." Women's History Matters, July 24, 2014. https://montanawomenshistory.org/contributions-of-a-mother-and-daughter/. Accessed April 27, 2022.
- Baumler, Ellen. "Mamie and Octavia Bridgewater and Montana's African American Community." *Beyond Schoolmarms and Madams: Montana Women's Stories.* Martha Kohl, ed. Montana Historical Society Press, 2016.
- Baumler, Ellen. Personal telephone conversation, May 17, 2022.
- "District Four Nurses Name Officers, Board." Helena *Independent Record,* March 4, 1956.
- Farley, Carolyn. "Black and White." Helena *Independent Record,* April 18, 2000.
- Hampton, Kate. Email communication, May 31, 2022.
- Hanshew, Annie. "'Lifting as We Climb': The Activism of the Montana Federation of Colored Women's Clubs." Women's History Matters website by the Montana Historical Society, https://montanawomenshistory.org/lifting-as-we-climb-the-activism-of-the-montana-federation-of-colored-womens-clubs/. Accessed April 27, 2022.
- Harrell-Campbell, Janet, and Dr. Jules Harrell. Personal telephone conversation, October 4, 2019, and conversations in spring 2022.

- Hilander, Sally. "Helena Native Has Roots Galore." Helena *Independent Record*, December 9, 1979.
- Munger, Mary. "Octavia Bridgwater is promoted to First Lieutenant." In "In Yesterday's News, In Tribute to Captain Octavia Bridgwater," May 27, 1945; believed to have been published in the Montana Nurses Association newsletter. Montana Historical Society vertical file.
- "Negro Nurse Enrolls in Red Cross Nursing Service." Helena *Independent Record*, October 4, 1942.
- Octavia Bridgwater obituary. Helena *Independent Record*, December 13, 1985.
- "Race Relations in the 1930s and 1940s." U.S. History Primary Source Timeline. Library of Congress. https://www.loc.gov/classroom-materials/united-states-history-primary-source-timeline/great-depression-and-world-war-ii-1929-1945/race-relations-in-1930s-and-1940s/.
- Robison, Kenneth G. "Breaking Racial Barriers, Civil Rights Movements in Montana and Wyoming." *Black Americans and the Civil Rights Movement in the West.* Bruce A. Glasrud and Cary D. Wintz, eds. University of Oklahoma Press, 2019.
- Supplementary Listing Record, Haight-Bridgewater House. National Register of Historic Places, NRIS Reference Number: 14000080 Haight-Bridgewater House. https://npgallery.nps.gov/GetAsset/f7cd09ac-a453-4634-9105-787d52b3b726/.
- Williams, Charnan. "The Bridgwater Family: A History of an African American Family in the American West from Slavery to the Civil Rights Era." *Western Historical Quarterly*, Vol. 51 (Winter 2020). Oxford University Press on behalf of the Western History Association.

CHAPTER 9—ELOUISE COBELL

- Bullock, Steve. Letter and attachments of Montana heroes to U.S. Secretary of Interior David Bernhardt, advocating Cobell be considered for honors and a statue in the National Garden, August 28, 2020. Copy of correspondence from Office of the Governor, Montana, August 28, 2020.
- Coleman, Travis. "Blackfeet Woman's Battle for Trust Settlement Long, Pitched." *Great Falls Tribune*, January 3, 2010.
- Department of Interior Blog, "10 Quotes of Reflection from Elouise Cobell About the Historic Cobell Settlement." https://www.doi.gov/blog/10-quotes-reflection-elouise-cobell-about-historic-cobell-settlement.

- Ferguson, Laura. "Elouise Pepion Cobell: Banker-Warrior." *Beyond Schoolmarms and Madams: Montana Women's Stories*. Edited by Martha Kohl, Montana Historical Society Press, 2016.
- Friends Committee on National Legislation. "Native American Trust Fund: Massive Mismanagement." September 29, 2016. https://www.fcnl.org/updates/2016-09/native-american-trust-fund-massive-mismanagement.
- Harleston, Robb. "Indian Trust Lands Lawsuit." Interview with Elouise Cobell, *Washington Journal*, C-SPAN, April 12, 2006. C-span.org/video/?192017-4/Indian-trust-lands-lawsuit.
- Hevesi, Dennis. "Elouise Cobell, 65, dies; sued U.S. over Indian trust funds." *The New York Times*, October 17, 2011.
- "Indian Leader Elouise Cobell Dies." *The Telegraph*, October 16, 2011.
- Janko, Melinda. "100 Years: One Woman's Fight for Justice." In *America ReFramed*, World channel, season 6, episode 4. https://worldchannel.org/episode/arf-100-years/. Accessed October 30, 2021.
- Janko, Melinda. "Elouise Cobell: A Small Measure of Justice." *American Indian*, Smithsonian's National Museum of the American Indian, Summer 2013, Vol. 14, No. 2.
- "Joint Commission to Investigate Indian Affairs." Committee on Indian Affairs, 63rd U.S. Congress, February 20, 1915.
- Judy, Beth. "Elouise Pepion Cobell: Accounting for Justice." *Bold Women in Montana History*. Mountain Press, 2017.
- Kennedy, J. Michael. "Truth and Consequences on the Reservation." *Los Angeles Times*, July 7, 2002.
- Kline, Alan. "An Indian Banker's Lifelong Crusade." *American Banker*, November 23, 1998. Land Buy-Back Program for Tribal Nations. U.S. Department of the Interior. https://www.doi.gov/buybackprogram.
- Maas, Peter. "She Seeks Justice." *Parade*, insert with the Helena *Independent Record*, September 9, 2001.
- Moss, Jamie. "$3.4+ Billion Settlement Announced in Federal Mismanagement of Individual Indian Trust." Indian Trust Settlement, December 9, 2009. http://www.indiantrust.com/pressrelease.html.

- Norris, Michelle. "Plaintiff in Indian Case on Settlement." *All Things Considered*, National Public Radio, December 8, 1994. https://www.npr.org/templates/story/story.php?storyId=121216148.
- Puckett, Karl. "Indians Extol Hard-fought Trust Victory." *Great Falls Tribune*, January 16, 2011.
- Ratledge, Mark. "The Burial of Elouise Cobell." *High Country News*, November 28, 2011.
- Rothberg, Emma. "Elouise Cobell ("Yellow Bird Woman")." National Women's History Museum, 2020. https://www.womenshistory.org/education-resources/biographies/elouise-cobell-yellow-bird-woman. Accessed July 17, 2021.
- Sonnenberg, Susanna. "From Ghost Town to Growing Community: Browning Banker Brings Business Back to the Reservation." *Montana Business Quarterly*, September 22, 1997.
- Szpaller, Keila. "Cobell Speech Inspires, Shames." *Great Falls Tribune*, July 4, 2005.
- Whitty, Julia. "Accounting Coup." *Mother Jones*, September/October 2005.

CHAPTER 10—MINNIE TWO SHOES

- Associated Press. "25th Anniversary of '73 Wounded Knee Occupation Draws Many." *Wotanin Wowapi*, March 5, 1998.
- Blakemore, Erin. "The Radical History of the Red Power Movement's Fight for Native American Sovereignty." *National Geographic*, November 25, 2020. https://www.nationalgeographic.com/history/article/red-power-movement-radical-fight-native-american-sovereignty?loggedin=true. Accessed April 6, 2022.
- Carmichael, Taté (Minnie Two Shoes' daughter). Telephone conversation, May 18, 2022.
- "Characteristics of American Indians by Tribes and Selected Areas: 1980." 1980 Census of Population, Bureau of the Census, U.S. Department of Commerce, PC80-1-2C, September 1989.
- DeMain, Paul. Email correspondence, March 31, April 16, April 25, and April 30, 2022.

- DeMain. Telephone interview, March 30, 2022.
- Ferguson, Laura. "Minnie Two Shoes: American Indian Journalist." Women's History Matters, Montana Historical Society. https://montanawomenshistory.org/minnie-two-shoes-american-indian-journalist/. Accessed April 2, 2022.
- Gease, Heidi Bell. "Annie Mae Aquash: 34 Years After Her Body was Found in the Badlands, Pieces of Murder Mystery Come Together." *Rapid City Journal*, November 28, 2010.
- Giago, Tim. "The Ugliest Car on the Reservation." *LaCrosse Tribune*, February 8, 2006.
- Hardin, Leslie. "Anachronisms Remind Woman of Roots." Springfield [Missouri] *News-Leader*, January 15, 1989.
- Hinchman, Steve. "Media on the Reservation." *Sacramento Bee*, August 28, 1988.
- Kades, Deborah. "Native Hero." *Wisconsin Academy Review*, Winter 2005.
- Landry, Alysa. "Native History: AIM Occupation of Wounded Knee Begins." *Indian Country Today*, February 27, 2017.
- Leibowitz, Barry. "Killer of Annie Mae Aquash, American Indian Activist, Gets Life Sentence." CBS News, January 25, 2011. https://www.cbsnews.com/news/killer-of-annie-mae-aquash-american-indian-activist-gets-life-sentence/. Accessed April 23, 2022.
- Littlefield, Daniel. Telephone interview, April 21, 2022.
- Martin, Catherine Anne. "The Spirit of Annie Mae." National Film Board of Canada, 2002.
- McKosato, Harlan. "AIM Disinformation." *Native American Calling* transcript by Southpaw Media, Native American Public Telecommunications, November 3, 1999.
- Mentzer, Rob. "The Messenger: Publisher Ran Native American Paper 33 Years." Wisconsin Public Radio and Eau Claire *Leader-Telegram*. November 8, 2019.
- NAJA Journalists, Video interview of Richard Two Elk, re: Arlo Looking Cloud early in the investigation, believed to be 1998.
- "Remembering Minnie Two Shoes." Indian Country TV, April 9, 2010. https://www.youtube.com/watch?v=FWtKMQb7a-Q. Accessed May 22, 2022.

- Schumann, Sada. "Minnie Two Shoes: Activist and Journalist." https://www.youtube.com/watch?v=u0uxctdoosU.
  Made when Sada was 13, a student at Sacajawea Middle School in Bozeman (based on interviews with historian Laura Ferguson and journalist Paul DeMain).
- Two Shoes, Minnie. "Red Road Home: Earning a Name." *Wotanin Wowapi*, May 13, 1999.
- Two Shoes, Minnie. "Statement by Minnie Two Shoes, re: Conversation With Iris Thunder Cloud on Anna Mae Pictou Aquash and AIM." *News From Indian Country*, February 5, 2002.
- Two Shoes, Minnie. "Where is Minnie Two Shoes?" *Wotanin Wowapi*, March 25, 2004.
- Two Shoes, Minnie. Untitled "Red Road Home" on choosing Indian tacos. *Wotanin Wowapi*, no date.
- Washines, Ronnie. "Minnie Two Shoes." *Native Times*, April 14, 2010.
- Worthington, Peter. "Will Justice Be Served?" *Windsor Star*, June 19, 1999.

Index

Page numbers in **bold** indicate illustrations.

A

B

C

D

E

F

G

H

I

J

N

O

P

R

S

T

U

V

W

Y

About the Author

PHOTOGRAPHY COURTESY OF THE HELENA *INDEPENDENT RECORD.*

MARGA LINCOLN IS A FREELANCE WRITER and former regional, education, and arts reporter for the *Independent Record* in Helena, Montana.

She was drawn to community journalism as a way to tell everyday people's stories. Why did they become passionate about playing Mozart concertos? Or create gigantic surrealistic sculptures in their backyard? Or write Montana novels set in turn-of-the-century Butte? Or labor to create a world-class ceramic arts center in rural Montana? The people she met inspired her because they poured their energy into their passions regardless of the personal costs.

In other cases, it was trying to capture the story and emotions that drove citizens to show up en masse at a school board meeting or a county commission meeting.

These are the people that reflect the character of our Montana towns.

The saying goes that journalism is just the rough draft of history. So, for Marga, writing the rough draft made her curious to dig deeper, to audit history classes at Carroll College, and to look back in time to find courageous, everyday people and listen to what they have to say to us today.

Marga earned an MS degree in agricultural journalism at the University of Wisconsin-Madison, where she worked as a science writer and editor before moving to Montana.

An award-winning arts and education reporter, she most cherishes a NAMI Montana Hero award, a Meloy Stevenson Award of Distinction from the Archie Bray Foundation, and the fact that she got to spend years of her life writing about hundreds of inspiring, everyday people.

She is married to free spirit and soul mate, John Hoffland. They have one adult daughter, Rosa, and two very lively grandsons, Theo and Mattias, who are daily reminders of why these people and stories matter now and for years to come.

Other Montana Books by Farcountry Press

Heroes of the Bob Marshall Wilderness
by John Fraley
978-1-56037-774-0
$17.95

Montana Battlefields, 1806–1877
Native Americans and the U.S. Army at War
by Barbara Fifer
978-1-56037-309-4
$14.95

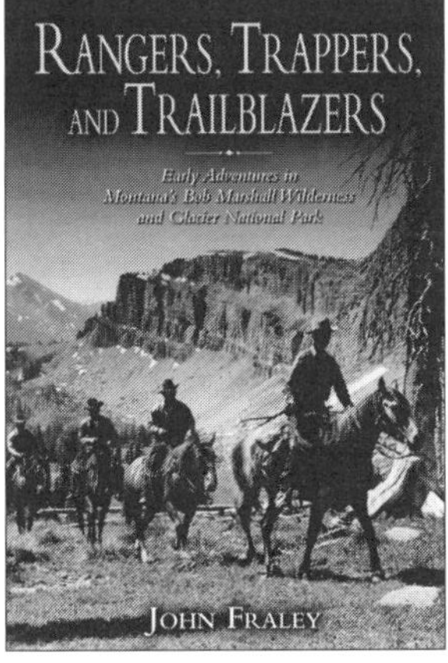

Rangers, Trappers, and Trailblazers
Early Adventures in Montana's Bob Marshall Wilderness and Glacier National Park
by John Fraley
978-1-56037-732-0
$16.95

Montana Women Homesteaders
A Field of One's Own
edited by Sarah Carter
978-1-56037-449-7
$17.95

The Kemptons
Adventures of a Montana Ranch Family, 1880–1964
by Trudy Kempton Dana
978-1-56037-733-7
$17.95

Splendid Was The Trail
by Kenneth D. Swan
978-1-56037-816-7
$16.95

More Montana Campfire Tales
Fifteen Historical Narratives
by Dave Walter
978-1-56037-236-3
$7.95

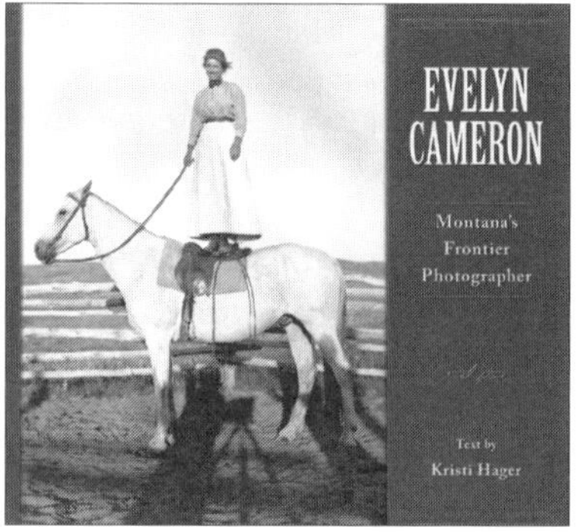

Evelyn Cameron
Montana's Frontier Photographer
text by Kristi Hager
978-1-56037-465-7
$16.95

West to Montana
A Saga of Homesteading on Tough Creek
by Christine Wortman-Engren
978-1-56037-697-2
$19.95

Vigilante Days and Ways
by Nathaniel P. Langford
foreword by Dave Walter
978-1-56037-038-3
$14.95

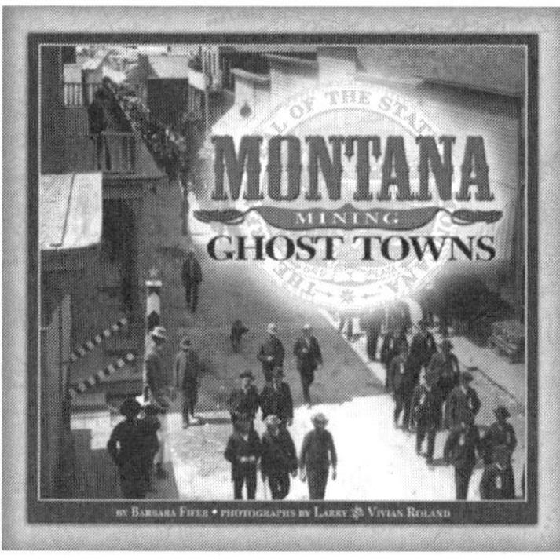

Montana Mining Ghost Towns
by Barbara Fifer
photography by
Larry and Vivian Roland
978-1-56037-779-5
$19.95

Montana Madams
by Nann Parrett
978-1-56037-634-7
$16.95

Montana Disasters
True Stories of Treasure State Tragedies and Triumphs
by Butch Larcombe
978-1-56037-776-4
$18.95

Death & Survival in Glacier National Park
True Tales of Tragedy, Courage, & Misadventure
by C. W. Guthrie &
Dan and Ann Fagrex
978-1-56037-658-3
$18.95

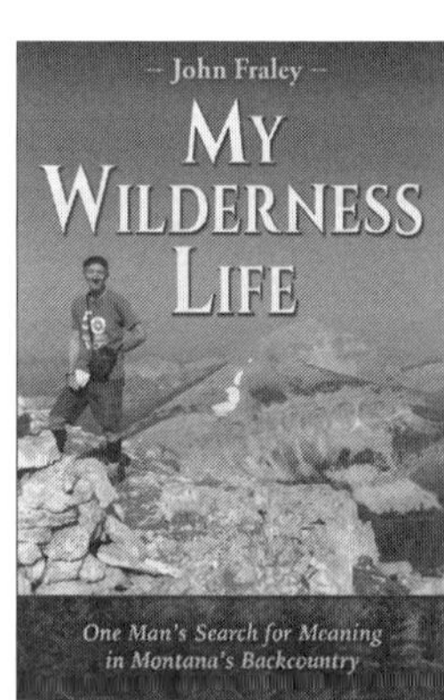

My Wilderness Life
One Man's Search for Meaning in Montana's Backcountry
by John Fraley
978-1-56037-822-8
$19.95

A Woman's Way West
In and Around
Glacier National Park,
1925 to 1990
by John Fraley
978-1-56037-762-7
$16.95

Wild River Pioneers
Adventures in the Middle
Fork of the Flathead,
Great Bear Wilderness and
Glacier National Park
by John Fraley
978-1-56037-794-8
$22.95

Montana's Indians
Yesterday & Today
text by William L. Bryan, Jr.
photography by
Michael Crummett
978-1-56037-064-2
$30.00

First Rangers
The Life and Times of
Frank Liebig and Fred Herrig,
Glacier Country, 1902–1910
edited by C. W. Guthrie
978-1-56037-749-8
$14.95

Glacier National Park
The First 100 Years
by C. W. Guthrie
978-1-56037-336-0
$39.95

Glacier's Historic
Hotels & Chalets
View with a Room
by Ray Djuff and Chris Morrison
foreword by Louis F. Hill
978-1-56037-556-2
$19.95

A Taste of Montana
Favorite Recipes from Big Sky Country
by Seabring Davis
foreword by Greg Patent
photography by Paulette Phlipot
978-1-56037-819-8
$26.95

Good Montana Morning
Recipes from Good Medicine
Lodge in Whitefish, Montana
by Betsy Cox
photography by Megan DiTizio
978-1-59152-075-7
$19.95

Glacier Country
Montana's Glacier National Park,
by R.C. Bert Gildart,
David Alt, C.W. Buchholtz,
and Bob Frauson
978-1-56037-811-2
$18.95

Montana Moments
photography by Chuck Haney
978-1-56037-703-0
$32.95

Glacier Day Hikes
Revised Edition
by Alan Leftridge
978-1-56037-823-5
$16.95

The Best of Glacier National Park
by Alan Leftridge
978-1-56037-560-9
$19.95

Glacier
A Photographic Journey
photography and text by
Zack Clothier
and Stephen C. Hinch
978-1-56037-740-5
$14.95

Montana
A Photographic Journey
photography by Stephen C. Hinch
and Jason Savage
978-1-56037-702-3
$14.95

Born Wild in Montana
photography and text by
Donald M. Jones
978-1-56037-487-9
$14.95

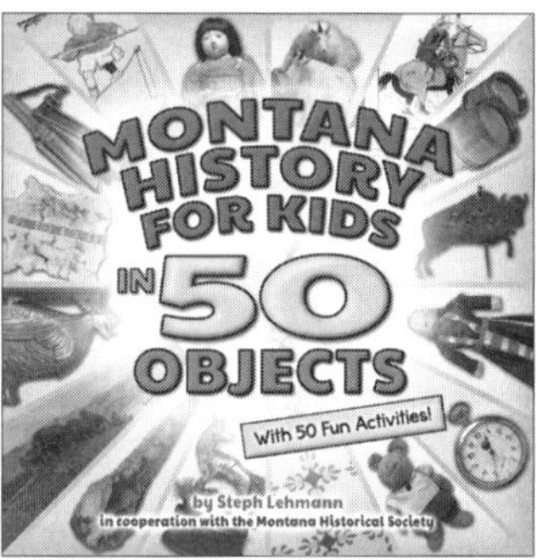

Donald M. Jones' Wild Montana
photography and text by
Donald M. Jones
978-1-56037-709-2
$26.95

Montana Chillers
13 True Tales of
Ghosts and Hauntings
by Ellen Baumler
illustrations by
Robert Rath
978-1-56037-496-1
$12.95

Montana History for Kids in 50 Objects
With 50 Fun Activities!
by Steph Lehmann
in cooperation with the
Montana Historical Society
978-1-56037-789-4
$18.95